THE
THREE GAMES
OF
SELLING

VOSS W. GRAHAM

To Robin,
My life companion, business partner and spiritual guru.
Thanks for allowing me to be me. All those hours watching
college football finally paid off with this book - which com-
bines my two major passions of business to business selling
and college football.

Also, a very special thanks to my daughter - Jennifer.
She was tenacious in encouraging me to finish this book.
And, she designed the cover for this book - a grateful
thanks.

Finally, thanks to my son - Voss, Jr.
He has demonstrated the power of having passion about
what you do!

Three Games of Selling   Copyright - 2006 by Voss W. Graham

Published by: uGrow Publishing,   Memphis, Tennessee
First Printing, 2006

Printed in the United States of America

ISBN-13: 978-0-9788045-1-0
ISBN-10: 0-9788045-1-1

Library of Congress number applied for.

For more information about Voss W. Graham or InnerActive Consulting Group, Inc., please visit us on the web at www.inneractiveconsulting.com or VossGraham.com or call 1-901-757-4434

Check out www.threegamesofselling.com for additional articles, CD's and guides for sales success.

Contents

Forward

After years of working with sales people, marketing people, vice presidents of sales, and CEO's, I began to view the world of selling as a form of mini-war. Sometimes the battle existed between the marketing and sales departments as well as the more standard battle with the competition. Simple methods for success in selling became complex, and, on a daily basis, non-sales oriented personnel challenged the abilities of sales people.

As I began to look at the situation, it became evident that there needed to be a way for more people to actually relate to selling and to how sales people win in this complex and, sometimes, hostile world.

Thus I began to look for ways to make associations or analogies that would assist people in learning the keys for selling success and how to develop a world-class sales organization.

The world of sports showed promise as an analogy to the everyday association to the requirement for sales success. Therefore, I set out to make it easier for individuals to learn the most important aspects for selling success, and to put them into an easy to remember format – like the games we play – especially the contact sport of football. Some of the greatest sales people, leaders, and coaches of people have come from the world of football.

Game One

Inner Game of Selling

Introduction

Everything starts with your mindset

Part one of this book covers the Inner Game of Selling, where we show how our mindset impacts our selling success. Just like Notre Dame had the Four Horseman that led the team to the National Championship, we have the Four Horsemen of Self. Each one is different and unique, yet, in the mental make-up of individuals, they need to be working together to enhance your overall success.

The First Horseman of Self is about Self-Awareness. This is the starting point for all personal leadership. Each person needs to become aware of his or her own natural strengths and weaknesses, and fully recognize how to utilize their strengths. The next step is to determine the weaknesses that will have a detrimental impact upon their career. If it is important to their success, then they need to learn how to improve it – sooner, rather than later. If it is not important to the success of the job, then don't worry about it and focus upon your strengths and get started on your career.

The Second Horseman that we will explore is Self-

Concept. This is a key factor in that it shows how you look at yourself and how you derive your personal expectations. If you are too tough on yourself, you can damage your self-esteem, which leads to negative emotions and feelings of victimhood taking over your mindset. In later chapters, we will explore, in depth, the ramifications of the power of self-concept upon your sales success.

The Third Horseman is Self-Confidence. This one concept when ignored or left unattended will lead to fluctuating performance levels. By focusing on improving one's self-confidence, you will become a major player in your industry. Why? Because customers want to work with people who are confident – people that they can be confident in for consistent levels of performance, or that bring the "get it done" mentality to the sales game.

The Fourth Horseman of Self is Self-Mastery, which is very unique, due to the level of work you have to apply to reach that level. When you have self-mastery, you recognize several key factors. One, it takes continued effort to maintain Mastery. Two, the more you learn – the more you learn that there is more to learn! This becomes a major breakthrough in becoming a skilled master of selling.

Chapter One

The Horseman of Self-Awareness

The starting point for every leadership process we have seen, read about, or participated in, was self-awareness of our strengths and weaknesses. Now this is not just about your intelligence or IQ, it is about how and why you do the things you do on a regular basis. It is about your personal behavioral style preferences and the things that you value in life. Knowing what makes you tick and being fully aware of these traits and factors that influence your priorities and behavior, allows you to take more control of your life and performance.

Let's start by learning about behavioral style fundamentals. Your personal behavioral style has been with you for a long time, and while some say that it is hard-wired in your brain, I believe that we have certain levels of comfort regarding "how" we do things and we attempt to simplify our lives by using a primary behavioral style on a daily basis. I say this because, as humans, we can choose to use different behaviors whenever we choose to do so – however, using a secondary behavioral style can lead to personal stress, if we use it for long periods of time. If our job requires us to use a secondary behavioral style everyday, then we will become so stressed that after eighteen to twenty four months – we quit, get a transfer, or get fired. Why? Because if we have mismatched our strengths and weaknesses to a job that requires us to suppress our strengths and use our weaknesses, we will become stressed and burn out very quickly. What a mess! Yet, people enter the sales profession on a daily basis where the position expects a certain type of behavioral style and these people are adapting their style to meet these expectations. Then as the stress heightens, turnover and burnout become more common.

So, how do we overcome this stress issue? We learn about our personal behavioral style through a quality assessment that gives you objective data about your style, your motivators, and other in-depth patterns relative to personal skills and attributes. This type of information will assist you in choosing a position that allows you to operate from a pattern of strength rather than a pattern of weakness.

The best coaches in football understand the value of quality behavioral assessments. They are using these assessments to understand the make-up of each player on the team and how to motivate and communicate with each player. This practice is also utilized by the top sales managers, who want to know how to manage and communicate with every person on their team. The old tactic of managing everyone the same is no longer a viable method to maximize performance or tap into pure potential of individual sales people.

Jimmy Johnson (College and Professional Coach) used these assessments to learn each person's natural strengths and weaknesses and coached each person according to their needs rather than his needs. The results of this coaching technique was a complete turnaround of one college team, a couple of national championships at another college, and he topped this off with a couple of Super Bowl wins!

As a sales person, knowing your behavioral style will allow you to understand the proper course to take when dealing with customers that have different styles than you. The ability to flex your behavioral style requires you to first understand your style. There are four core elements within the behavioral styles' patterns or profiles. As you review the next section, consider which behavioral style is more like you and which behavioral style is like a specific client. Then begin to consider the keys to relating to the different behavioral styles.

The first one is a person who is aggressive, results oriented, direct, task oriented, demanding, and very business-like in dealing with issues. Sometimes quick to anger, they are loud and only focused upon getting the results they want. If you are dealing with this type of customer, then you must be prepared, focused and bottom line oriented. Since they value results and are fast paced, you do not waste their time with idle chatter or family discussions – get right to the point with a summary presentation relating what benefits they will receive.

The second behavioral style is a person who is talkative, outgoing, friendly, direct, fast paced, more relationship oriented and possessing a need to be appreciated for who they are. This person appears to be friendly and will talk about themselves and the value they bring to the situation. They tend to "wing-it" and are big picture oriented and are not as detail conscious as others. When dealing with this person, take more time in building a relationship with him or her. It is important that this person likes you and feels that you are supportive of their role and goals. Be careful not to get carried away with the pinball thinking that this person uses or you will lose valuable time riding their dreams rather than getting a contract.

The third behavioral style is a person who is systematic, step-by-step, non-confrontational, easy going, relationship oriented and uses a slower pace. Their major theme is to "get along with others". These people are process-oriented and will answer a "why" question like it was a "how to" question. Often these people are very slow to make a decision, yet, be patient and never push this style since they will just say "no" to get rid of the pushy sales person! The key to dealing with this behavioral style is to slow down, build a trust based relationship (share information), and be aware that until they trust you, they will not give you any helpful hints or feedback to let you know where they are in the process. They are very safety conscious and will become aggressive if they feel that their job security is at risk due to your proposal. While they can get aggressive, it is usually the passive aggressive variety that they specialize in using on sales people.

The fourth behavioral style is a person who is accurate, detail oriented, task focused, critical, very time sensitive, factual, and concerned with quality of work. Their major theme is to get it right and everything they do follows this theme. These people will debate facts and details and enjoy it! They will be totally defensive if someone criticizes the quality of their work. Therefore, be very careful to focus upon the facts or details, and not the quality of their work. When dealing with this behavioral style, be aware that they will tend to be quiet and not offer any additional information that you need. Therefore, specific questions are important to uncover information for your sales solutions. Also, be prepared to support your comments with details, facts, and testimonials to prove your position. These people like proof since they are primarily risk averse.

While we have briefly discussed the big four core elements of behavioral style, you can have any combinations in your style. There is a primary behavioral style and usually people have one or two secondary cores in their pattern mix. However, you can always learn your personal behavioral style using a quality assessment tool. Once you understand your behavioral style, then you can learn methods of recognizing others' styles and applying flexibility to your selling style when it is appropriate. If you attempt to flex all day, then you are overly adapting and not honoring your natural behavioral style – leading to increased negative stress and lower performance levels.

What motivates you?

Another area of self-awareness concerns understanding the things that you value. The act of valuing something adds to your desire to execute and perform in ways that will enhance or deliver what you value. An example of this drive comes from the motivator that we call the Utilitarian Drive, or the need for a return on everything that we do including time, energy and effort. This is very important for a successful sales person. Without this drive a salesperson will be less focused upon results, deadlines, monthly and quarterly numbers. They would tend to lack the urgency for getting results, waiting for others to take action rather than taking action themselves.

People lacking this drive need to be honest with themselves, and seek out a job that has less demanding results orientation and a compensation system that is safe and fixed rather than a system with potential upside based upon getting greater results and sharing in the rewards using commissions.

Look for a good "business oriented" assessment tool to give you an objective look at your personal motivator package. A knowledgeable coach can explain the uniqueness that you possess and how your combination will support or depress your performance. Again, a key factor for consideration would be the traits and characteristics necessary for the job position to be successful. The closer the match between the job requirements and your personal talent traits is, the higher the probability of your long-term success.

> Inneractiveassessments.com is an excellent resource for personal and professional assessments.

Understanding what motivates you is important because you learn where you derive passion. When we have passion relative to what we do, then we become more focused as well as driven for results that support our needs. It also helps to know what areas we will be very indifferent or negative about, since to others these areas may be what they are passionate about. When people are engaged in communication, presentations, interviews, etc., their passions and indifferences can be heard loud and clear. If during a customer interaction, we find that the customer is passionate about something that we are indifferent to – it is our responsibility to avoid de-valuing their position or be prepared to engage in a very emotional dialogue concerning the reasons you should find value in their arena. These factors contain "hotspots" for natural tensions or debates, thus losing the effectiveness of our efforts, and, in a worst case, totally losing the trust of the customer.

Coach Voss's Chalk Talk

Chapter One: Self-Awareness

» *Starting point for achieving personal leadership*

» *Understanding behavorial style is a key tool to success*

» *Assessments give objective data to an individual - just like height, weight, strength measures and 40 yard sprint times are important to coaches and athletes*

» *Flexibility - like in football - is important to sales people. Flexibility of behavioral style is important to sales and communication success*

» *Personal priorities are the motivators that drive performance*

Chapter Two

The Horseman of Self-Concept

In the world of sports we have a unique situation regarding the top programs in that they expect to win every time, no matter what else is happening. The top player could be injured or having a bad day, or the weather could be bad, or the crowd could be hostile, yet, in the end the team finds a way to win. This is the winner's edge, and it begins in the mind of the players. They expect to win. Losers expect to lose or are focused on "what bad thing will happen that will cause us to lose?"

Are you focused upon winning or losing? Whichever is your answer, your mind will see to it that you are right! Since we know that your mental makeup has a significant influence on your personal performance, it is very important that you think like a winner.

An interesting thing about the differences between winners and losers, there is only minimal skill, competencies, or attributes gaps between the two classes; yet, the difference in results between the two classes is very significant. Since skills, competencies, and attributes can be measured, what is the factor that leads to such big differences in personal performance? It is simply the attitudes that people bring to the game. Attitude has a multiplier effect on both our inborn attributes like intelligence and behavioral style and our learned attributes of skills, knowledge, and experience. Using a positive multiplier, a person can distance themselves from both peers and competition relative to the results and outcomes – especially in the world of selling.

Our self-concept is the bundle of beliefs about everything that we are. It is a cumulative or composite effect of our beliefs as to just how good we are in all aspects of our life. Our self-concept impacts the most important part of our brains – the subconscious mind. The subconscious mind is our personal super computer that really controls our overall performance on a daily basis. This super computer operates on a program that we have designed and implemented during our lifetime. If you believe the old computer cliché of "garbage in – garbage out," then be very careful in how you program your mind since it will deliver on "your programs!"

The Law of Subconscious Activity works to ensure that your mental programs are followed and executed on a daily basis. Subconscious activity is the method of following your personal beliefs regarding how well you perform, what results you get, how you are perceived in the marketplace and what are your limits.

By self-programming our minds, we determine the limits of our success and what we are willing to do to achieve in life. This factor is in play in all facets of our life; yet, most studies have been in the areas of human performance. The research in high performance is very clear – it is the soft skills that are making the significant differences in performance levels. And an interesting footnote on this research is that high levels of intelligence or IQ show no direct correlation to high performance. Yet, I have to say that it is a handy thing to have in your toolbox. True intelligence has been defined as how well you apply knowledge. My experience shows that the ability of knowledge application is in demand in our marketplace today.

Another factor that comes into play concerning top performers is their ability to remain positive and optimistic no matter what is happening to them or in the marketplace. Again, research has shown in several cases that the ability to see the good in any situation allows for improved decision making and thus higher levels of performance. Optimism is a key factor for winners. It is not based upon blind faith or positive thinking. It is based upon learning new information with each situation that comes across our paths – looking for the lesson to be learned or the opportunity to go after. Too many people miss excellent opportunities because they are "bad mouthing" situations and feeling like victims that are totally out of control. No learning + No opportunities = little chance for advancement. Stay focused on moving forward and look for chances to excel.

Three Components of the Self-Concept

There are three components that impact our overall self-concept. The first of the three components is the concept of *self-ideal*. This is the vision part, whereby you create the description of the person you aspire to become. The more complete and detailed the description, the higher the probability that you will become this person. This happens due to the power of the sub-conscious mind that uses the law of subconscious activity to deliver your vision. Since the subconscious cannot sort the differences between truth and visions, it works to deliver on your programming. The actual truth is that you can be whatever your mind can conceive and believe. Therefore, the more details including color and action that you can place into your vision of your future ideal, the easier it is for you to become this person.

Let me take a moment to add one important concept in this segment, which is the difference between perfection and progress. Beware of the need to be perfect all the time. This thinking leads to negative attitudes, due to feelings of inadequacies, looking to blame something or some-one for deficiencies, being a victim of some event, and finally lowering your self-esteem. We need to learn to look for improvement in our performance, look at the gains we have achieved during a comparable time period, celebrate the improvements while looking for additional methods for future improvements. These activities allow us to feel like we have achieved goals. Performance improvement creates higher self-esteem and in turn we feel like we are responsible for our personal results.

High performers have a very clear vision of their self-ideal, and are constantly moving toward this vision. They tend to set higher standards for themselves and work hard to deliver upon their standards. This technique can and should be used on all aspects of your life. You can create your life and answer your lifestyle questions by clearly defining your self-ideal. Create a vision of your future state and aspire to achieve it on a daily basis.

Sadly, unsuccessful people and unsuccessful teams have no vision of their future and use the "law of accident" to move into the future. Just like winners truly believe in themselves and expect to win, losers truly believe that "stuff" will happen to knock them out of the winners' circle. By focusing and concentrating on the worst-case scenario, they attract into their lives the negative results they are focusing upon. Another negative side effect of having a fuzzy vision or no vision at all, is the lack of progress they make upon themselves. Due to the lack of understanding the differences between where they are today compared to where they should be according to their ideal list of qualities, the losers fail to improve and thus get stuck in comfort zones or habitual behaviors leading nowhere. Self-improvement dies along with the person's potential and the life attitude.

The second component of self-concept is our *self-image*. Self-image is the way that you think about yourself and see yourself in your mind's eye, as you go about performing your daily tasks and business. Some people describe the self-image as the mind's inner mirror – reflecting your perceptions of who you are and how well you will perform under specific circumstances. Again, the subconscious mind works hard to deliver upon your inner reflection of who you are and how well you perform.

The key thing about this self-image is that it is subjective in nature rather than an objective fact. Therefore, if we don't like the results that we are delivering today, then we can change our perception of who we are – thus, reprogramming our mental computer in line with who we aspire to be. We can improve our personal qualities and confidence quickly. As you change your self-image in a positive way, you will begin to see the differences in your performance and you will see and believe you have become more competent and capable as a sales person.

The final and third component of self-concept is *self-esteem*. Self-Esteem is how you feel about yourself. It is an emotional component and it has been proven to be the foundational piece for high performance. People with high personal self-esteem never take anything personally. Thus, they can successfully separate the business issues from their personal worth. People with lower levels of self-esteem will have a tendency to take business issues to a personal level. Thus, if a deal does not work out, they take on the concept of worthlessness. This feeling of worthlessness is a very destructive negative emotion and people who are affected by this feeling will tend to show negative emotions at the absolute wrong time and create additional problems leading to lower performance levels and increased feelings of worthlessness – sometimes this cycle leads a person to depression. Depression is the ultimate in low performance standards and can be a fatal blow to sales potential.

High self-esteem is the leading factor to overall happiness and success. Those who have developed and maintain their self-esteem at higher levels tend to accomplish more and live the lifestyle of THEIR CHOICE. They feel totally in control of their life and are capable of remaining calm in the face of any storm that appears.

Several people have shared with me one of the "secrets" to developing higher levels of self-esteem. The one that I hear most often is "learn to do your job very, very well". This feeling of self-efficacy allows people to know that they are capable of doing excellent work. The main factor they need to control is their attitude toward getting things done, learning what works and what needs improvement, and then doing something about the improvement. Losers have a tendency to wait for someone else to come along and "fix them." Self improvement coupled with action orientation is the bedrock for developing strong self-esteem. Strong self-esteem guides you into a future of success and achievement.

This is not to imply that people possessing high self-esteem have no crisis in their lives or no problems to deal with on a daily basis. They have the same number and types of crises and problems; yet, they understand that these are just external issues. They keep the external issues separate from their personal assessment of being a worthwhile human being. In other words, they know that they are "OK" and refuse to devalue themselves due to external influences. This healthy point of view allows high self-esteem people to deal with issues in an objective and positive way. "Solve the problem rather than being the problem" is their slogan in life.

Coach Voss's Chalk Talk

Chapter Two: Self-Concept

» *Winners believe they will win.*

» *A strong belief will create opportunities.*

» *The best sales people (and football players) find ways to win.*

» *Winners focus on the positives and look for lessons regarding negatives.*

» *Winning sales people have a long term vision for both performance and improvement.*

» *Learning how to do your job gives you the inner strength to deliver performance.*

» *Attitude of positive knowing allows you to have perserverance in the face of adversity.*

» *Winning is based upon individual choices along the pathway.*

Chapter Three

The Horseman of Self-Confidence

Self-confidence is the bedrock or foundational aspect for the successful athlete or salesperson. In fact, sales people with high levels of confidence seem to make sales before they even offer a solution. Why does this happen? Because customers want to do business with people with whom they are confident. They feel that these people will make things happen and will do whatever it takes to get the job done. People lacking self-confidence are at a clear disadvantage in the marketplace. Customers can sense a lack of confidence, and therefore lose faith in the abilities of the sales person. Yes, that is an emotional response by the customer. It is important to know that all decisions are based in emotional responses, and logic is used to justify our emotional decisions.

In the world of sports, confidence breeds a winners' attitude. They take control of their mental mindset and view all situations with a positive point of view. Losers tend to look for negatives and use both internal negative self-talk and external negative talk, which attracts more negative influences into their lives, and their results become a self-fulfilling prophecy.

The role of optimism is an important factor in both our self-confident point of view and how our customers view us. It all begins with how we talk to ourselves. If our primary view is one of optimism, then we will look for the good or the lesson to be learned in every situation. We will use positive self-talk to think about issues and how we will deal these issues in a positive way. The language that we should use with our customers has a positive and solution oriented sound. This is a primary method that winners use in dealing with both their thoughts and explanatory language. When telling their story to the customer, the language is positive and encouraging, which engages others in looking for more solutions and options for dealing with situations.

Losers tend to dwell on negative thoughts and how things cannot get done. Negative self-talk leads to self-limiting thoughts and a lack of alternatives or creativity for solving problems. This continuous stream of bad information causes the person to talk about why things will fail, and will negatively impact their confidence levels.

Listening to the players of continuously losing teams shows how the players have accepted the mental patterns of "I/we are not good enough to beat this team," or "Maybe we'll get lucky and upset them!" This type of talk shows a lack of confidence in the players and team to be a winner and expect to win in any game. The key here is a lack of commitment to making the best things happen. Another key element is the degree that individuals take responsibility for their actions.

Role of Commitment & Taking Responsibility

First, lack of commitment can be evident in both individuals and teams because the things that need to be done to ensure higher levels of success are overlooked. Lack of commitment is the killer of initiative. People tend to shy away from the activities such as training, practice and personal improvement because they feel that it will not matter; yet, everything counts! We can make a difference in what we do and especially in HOW we do it. Commitment to our own improvement and learning will lead the way to self-confidence. When we know that we can do things very well – we gain a degree of confidence over others that hesitate because they are not sure they can do it.

Second, taking responsibility is one of the most important elements in developing personal character. Closely related to being committed, taking responsibility shows a level of maturity that people need in order to be considered as competent. There are great athletes that should be All-Everything; yet, their performance becomes mediocre due to a lack of taking responsibility for their personal actions and comments. They lose the respect of teammates and their coaches. In other words, they are no longer counted upon to deliver the results of a winner. When people lose faith in someone, trust and respect are the targets for a downgrade.

People who take responsibility for their actions and their results become the "go to" people in tough games. Are you a go-to person?

There is a difference between a playmaker and an ego driven person. A playmaker is someone who has all the talent in the world and will make things happen in clutch situations.

They tend to excel in the tougher games against quality competition. The ego driven person may also have all the talent in the world and can make things happen – yet, the ego driven person is only in the game for themselves rather than the team. These people will do things to make themselves look good at game time. While they look good on paper, they make mistakes that cost the team the game. There are examples of these types of players in all sports. I watched an All-American wide receiver display the ego driven attitude in a bowl game several years ago. He was one of those game breaker types (i.e. great height, very fast and possessing all the statistics that fans love). However, in this game I watched him take a big hit in the first quarter and for the rest of the game he was short arming every pass thrown his way. Later, he told the press that he didn't want to get hurt in a meaningless game with his big payday coming in the pro draft.

Then, there is the opposite type of players that make a difference for their teams. While they are playmakers, they truly want the team to win and they are willing to do whatever it takes for their team to win – including downfield blocking, special teams and serious off season conditioning and strength programs. The writers who follow the pro teams have criticized one wide receiver that was recently drafted into the NFL. Yet, the insiders that know the true spirit, competitiveness and team player attitude of this particular person are excited to have him on their team. He will play on special teams and make tackles. He will block people so running backs can gain more yardage. And yes, he will catch everything thrown in his direction. Why? Because he takes responsibility for all his actions and believes that he is playing for the name on the side of helmet rather than the person in the helmet. What a winner he is and will be! (He made the All-Pro Rookie 1st Team.)

What are you willing to do to build your confidence?

There are several things you can do, including reprogramming your thoughts to the positive side. Many sales pros use affirmations to get themselves ready to perform at the highest level – when they are in front of the customer.

Another method is to plan your calls. The planning process alone allows for your confidence to build because you have a feeling of certainty about the call. Ambiguity and the fear of the unknown are major stress producers and are minimized by the best sales people through strategic and tactical planning.

Getting Results Faster for Sales people is a coaching workshop process that shows you how to control your own subconcsious beliefs that derive your performance standards. Learn how to improve your personal and professional life and see results immediately just by reformating your mind's hard drive into positive thinking.

For more information contact robin@gettingresultsfaster.com www.gettingresultsfaster.com

"Winging it" is for the losers. Can you imagine the impact of a football team if there was no offensive or defensive game plan! The quarterback is supposed to just make it up as he goes along. Without preparation, you lose the competitive advantage of knowing what to do in every potential situation. If you have no plan, any path will get you there.

Practice is another area that excellent sales people can gain confidence from before getting face to face with a customer. Yes, the common term is "role play." Since this term is so disliked by sales people, we use the term application exercises. Application exercises give you the opportunity to learn what to say, what tone of voice is best for total understanding, and how to answer that tough objection that has slowed you down in the past. There are so many things that you can improve, yet, just like the great athlete, you must practice the execution of your plays, your techniques, and your choices. Why do sales people dislike role plays? Because they could be seen doing something wrong! Well, what better time to get feedback as to how well you are doing something that can determine whether you win or lose? Your peers are your teammates, and they want you to win! Practice your trade so you can be the best in any situation. Your confidence will increase – why? Because you will know what to do and there will be no surprises.

Coach Voss's Chalk Talk

Chapter 3: Self-Confidence

» *Self confidence is a critical determinant for success.*

» *Self confidence is the wild card for winners - it allows them to trump others.*

» *Positive self talk leads to winning.*

» *Negative self talk leads to doubt, blame and losing.*

» *Lack of commitment kills initiative.*

» *Taking responsibility shows maturity and develops character.*

» *Character is a trait found in "real" winners.*

» *Have a plan - "winging it" is for losers.*

Chapter Four

The Horseman of Self-Mastery

Self-Mastery is a goal that most people long to attain, and yet, few actually get to this position. What is self-mastery? It is knowing that you can perform at very high levels within your selected profession. Another word for self-mastery is self-efficacy. Again, it is the knowledge you possess so you can perform any task within your current job and do it well.

How do you get to the status of self-mastery? Well, you must be willing to work hard in your profession. In other words, you must become a continual learner to get and stay at the top of your field. Some sales people confuse "getting to the next level" with their years of experience; claiming that they have x number of years of experience. However, in several cases the number of years has little to do with mastery of their profession. How can this happen? Because they haven't learned anything new since their first year in sales! These are the sales people that just go to the same people within their accounts for a visit, use the same techniques on everyone, and tell everyone (that will listen) that the reason their sales totals are not higher is "due to the high prices our managers force us to use," or some other excuse. When sales managers ask questions about these sales persons' accounts, it becomes evident that they really do not know very much about the customer, who the real influencers are, and what are their current issues and problems. Also there is little joint planning as to sales opportunities or product development needs. Why? Because the sales persons have not been aware that it is their responsibility to know more about the customer than the customer knows about themselves! The best sales people are always ahead of the curve in learning about their customers and in most cases their customer's customers.

The best sales people are continuous learners. The subjects for their learning are themselves, their customers, their industry, their techniques and strategy, and the business applications of their products and services, including the financial return on investments that their customer receives. They have a natural curiosity to learn more. I have witnessed this phenomenon over the past two decades – the top performers are always the first to sign up for new training and development. The losers say it is a waste of their time to go learn sales stuff because they already know it! This experience discloses the real reason that top sales people remain at the top of their field. They tell me that the more they learn, the more they discover they need to learn! In other words, they discovered that they did not know everything and needed to learn more to stay ahead.

This fact has become more evident as the experts have determined that overall information and knowledge is doubling every three years. When I first entered the business world, the velocity of knowledge growth was doubling every five to six years. You can see that this doubling effect is accelerating so learning is important just to maintain your existing knowledge level. Another way of looking at this reason for continuous learning is that for every year that passes, your personal knowledge bank is at risk of becoming one-third obsolete! What impact could that have on your performance if left unchecked?

One of the NFL's greatest wide receivers is Jerry Rice. If you were to shadow him during the year, you would learn how to get your body and mind ready to play the proper way. Rice has broken every receiving record in the NFL, and every catch and touchdown adds to his accomplishments and records. Yet, he is not a person who just shows up for the games and uses his experience from the first year of professional football. He is a continuous learner and practitioner of his profession. Before the season begins, he works hard at developing his strength and conditioning, so that he can deal with the new "20-somethings" that want to stop him from being successful. He also studies game film of his moves and techniques. He is looking for ways to improve and get a competitive advantage against younger and talented defensive backs. He also studies the different defensive formations that he will face during the year. Again, he is looking for weaknesses or clues for reading the exact coverages that he will be facing in games. Why does he do all this? Because he wants to perform at his best all the time. And he does.

How does this help you gain self-mastery? By learning from the best, you can benchmark best practices and master your profession. You can video yourself during application exercises and learn what needs to be improved, as well as what you are doing well, so that you can have the confidence to do what works with your customers.

Develop an attitude of the continuous learner. Read books written by the best sales professionals to gain insight into new or different methods for success. Remember that old saying – "leaders are readers!" Read a sales book every quarter and take notes on the important things you learned. This one practice alone will allow you to become an expert in the field of selling within three years. How? During a three-year period of reading books for the top sales experts, you will learn about the process of selling. Each writer has a different or unique focus; yet, you will learn that the sales processes within all these books are actually the same. Yet, due to the unique focus from each writer, you will learn how to understand each part of the sales process. When this happens you are well on your way to self-mastery.

There is another important lesson that can be learned as you move to self-mastery. The best sales people and the industry "super-stars" have learned that they cannot do everything alone. As they become more successful they have less free time to get everything done. They have to learn to collaborate with others, a sharing of tasks or activities. This allows the sales people to focus on what they do very well and let others do the things that they do best. This bond is called interdependency, and it is the highest stage of personal development that you can master.

There are a series of steps that a person must go through to successfully get to the level of interdependency. It is not an automatic thing that occurs because you 'will' it to be.

There is a process of human growth that starts with you being dependent upon others for your success. Usually in the sales field, this is your sales manager or another sales

Interdependency

Level that truly successful people choose to reach. Collaborates with others to leverage results to higher levels. Excellent communicators can motivate others in joint projects

Independency

Level that first stage high performers achieve. Knowing they can perform the tasks and functions of higher results. They get things done one by one, however lack leverage.

Dependency

Level that most people reside.
Look to others for direction and approval.

person who has been assigned to mentor you. You should have numerous unanswered questions for the person that you depend upon to teach you about your company, the policies, the politics, the products or services you sell, pricing, techniques, etc. The list is long in the beginning since you have little personal experience or specific knowledge. During this period of time, customers can be very scary people because they will ask questions that sound like they are in some foreign language when you hear them. This is a normal learning time in the sales person's timetable and the interesting thing is that the sales person is most open to new information and suggestions for improved performance. During this time period, the sales person actually learns more and executes as he or she is told and will begin to actually see growth in their sales and sales success stories. And as an individual becomes more experienced and successful - there is usually a move to the next level – independence.

The process of learning usually slows during this stage of the human growth cycle, as the feelings of "I already know that!" begin to creep into responses to opportunities for new learning. Yes, they are more experienced and knowledge-able. They demonstrate handling their territory and their customers with various degrees of success. There is a feeling of mastery of sales, and ego can get heavily involved in the person's attitude. While there is a big need for confidence in sales, ego can be a different animal in human performance. The bigger the ego, usually the lower the self-esteem. This is difficult for sales people to understand at times, yet it is a truth that has been verified in several studies on human performance. Remember you want a higher level of self-esteem so you can perform at higher levels of achievement. People with low self-esteem have major difficulties when situations get more complex which requires more confidence, calmness and purposeful actions.

Some sales people get to this level and remain here until retirement or just leave the sales profession. In fact, it would be safe to say that most sales people decide to stay in this level, or in an organization that nurtures the traditional "lone wolf" sales environment. In the latter case, the sales person may never learn that a higher level even exists, unless committed to a personal continuous learning process. There are some situations where the company, or organization that the sales person has been working in, begins to change the way they sell or go into the market. Sometimes it is a new and enlightened Vice President of Sales who discovers the third level. A decision is made in order for the company to grow, the sales team has to learn another way of selling rather than the independent lone wolf style of the traditional sales force.

Thus, the third level comes into play for sales professionals seeking a higher level of sales productivity. This third level is interdependency. The sales person has learned that as an independent sales person he or she cannot leverage sales success. Meaning a sales person feels a need to be involved in every sales transaction and order. Therefore, sales happen one by one rather than two by one, three by one, ten by one or even greater points of leverage. Another reason for the interdependency level is the need for team selling in larger, more complex selling situations. One person cannot know all the answers or be in several locations at the same time. Thus, this is the reason that sales people need to move to the next level - interdependency.

Interdependency is what makes great teams great! Each person on the team knows their assignments and takes responsibility for their areas on the field. Let's look at a football team to gain insight into what happens with great teams. First, the team has excellent athletes at all positions, the athletes have learned the system that the team uses (offensive systems and defensive systems) and have practiced the techniques to make every offensive play execute against different defensive alignments. Each individual is responsible for executing his personal assignment to make the play work well. When everyone is on the same page, the result is positive yardage for the offense. When executed at an excellent level there is a longer gain or a touchdown. There must be a confidence that everyone will handle his assignment as expected. The quarterback makes assignments, the lineman adjusts their blocking schemes, the wide receivers run the correct routes, and the running backs go to the right location or hole. This sounds complex and it is! Yet, the plays work well because there is a trust based confidence that every player will do his job on every play. And if the execution is at a high level, there will be positive results for the football team.

Now the best teams have this interdependency principle from the coaches to the players to the support staffs. The poor and mediocre teams are missing this interdependency part of the process. They usually have a number of independent types that do not play very good team ball. And due to this missing element, the team does not win often, does not play for the conference championship and definitely does not play for the national championships. The best teams have the best playmakers that are playing for the name on the helmet rather the person in the helmet.

Sales people who are serious about moving to the higher level of interdependency must be prepared to leave their egos at home. They need to be trusting of others and have positive expectations that others will, and can, perform at high levels. This is a team effort. It is true that you will have to work with others who are less experienced or less motivated than you are from time to time; yet, it is your responsibility to create an environment of positive expectations and a helpful attitude. I have met very few people who have stated that they want to do a lousy job today! What I have found is most people truly want to perform at high levels. The key for the sales person is to create a motivated climate when teaming up with others. Always keep focused on the purpose and objectives of the team – to win.

This interdependency level is necessary for sales teams to be effective in the worlds of joint ventures, true partnerships with customers and the newer collaborative style of effective selling. Also, if you are engaged in selling through distributors, the need for interdependency is critical. You need to coordinate efforts with the distributor and their sales teams, as well as the end user that you want asking for your specific products and services. It can be a balancing act of priorities; yet, with high levels of self-esteem and a true understanding of interdependency, you can leverage your results and gain a significant competitive advantage.

In summary, your level of self-mastery is in your hands. Be aware of how your self-talk helps or hinders your confidence to master your profession. No one else can give you self-confidence or self-mastery. It's all about the choices you can make regarding your future. Allow yourself the freedom to execute new things, experiment with new methods, learn from your mistakes, and modify your delivery. All of these actions will lead you to higher levels of self-mastery.

Coach Voss's Chalk Talk

Chapter Four: Self-Mastery

» *Experience does not equal high performance.*

» *Knowledge alone is good - knowing how and when to apply your knowledge is better.*

» *Continuous learning is the real key to improvement.*

» *Less effective performers are usually dependent upon someone else to give direction.*

» *High self ego's lead to self-centered attitudes with self interest decisions overcoming team goals.*

» *Collaboration and team focused decision make great teams.*

» *Greatness is directly linked to choices made.*

Game Two

The Active Game of Selling

Introduction

Selling is a Contact Sport

Part two covers the active game of selling, where we show how sales is a contact sport that requires an active engagement with people on a daily basis. While there are people that believe you can wait for the customers to call you, this is a myth! Passive activities will allow the competition to get a foothold and increase their chances of winning.

There are two primary considerations in the active game of selling. The first is the need to learn the best methods for executing excellent communication skills. In football, contact is all about blocking and tackling, hitting and avoiding being hit; the active game of selling is different. In selling, the active phase is contacting our customers and successfully communicating our message while building mutual confidence, rapport, and trust. The key is to actively engage the customer in the sales process and the customer's buying process. Always remember that involvement drives commitment. Therefore, if you are doing all the talking, then the customer is passive and you will lose more than you should.

We will look at three areas of improving your communication techniques in Chapter Five. The first includes using the fine art of questioning to gain a competitive advantage. Then the second area for improvement involves learning how the customer makes their buying decisions and what are their preferred methods in the buying process. And finally we will look at some of the basics of communication that lead to consistency and ultimately more success.

The second primary area that we will look at is the practicality of using a basic football tool – practice. The use of practice is a standard operational tool that is used in every sport. Why do sales people tend to shy away from this very useful and important habit? Only the sales people know the real reasons, yet the main reasons are believed to be the fear of failure and being seen by their peers as anything less than perfect in their performance and knowledge. While these two factors are housed in the mental makeup of an individual, the fastest way to overcome these blockers to rapid improvement is to actively engage in practice. Practice allows us to change bad habits and create new excellent habits without hurting us in the real world.

So in Chapter 6 on practice, we will be looking at the reasons for a personal kaizen approach. *Kaizen* means continuous improvement, and is a valid practice for people who want to become the very best in their profession. The second area to review is the use of application exercises as a tool for immediate feedback without losing a customer in the process of learning. The final area in the field of practice is looking at the use of video. College football teams and players are using this great tool to learn exactly what techniques are working and not working, and what are their natural strengths and weaknesses. The best thing about the use of video is the immediacy of feedback and the simplicity of seeing how you are actually performing your techniques.

Chapter Five

Actively Engaging Others

Winning football teams master the art of contact. The top teams want to dominate their opponent with aggressive and smart techniques. Passive teams usually get beat due to the physical pounding they take during the game. In the world of selling we cannot physically pound on our customers or prospects (even if we really want to with some of them!). Therefore, we must redirect this energy into the active game of communication skills. Our success depends upon our ability to engage the customer in conversations, which allow the customer to discover that our solution is the best solution. In order to be successful at this activity, we must learn the best practices of uncovering the customer's true needs and wants. Then, and only then, can we begin to offer our solutions for their improvement.

How much communication is going on in a football game? Actually, there is constant communication during the game. The offense has the quarterback calling out signals at the line of scrimmage. He is telling the team about the defensive alignment. If he sees a defense that is positioned to stop the play that was called in the huddle, then he calls an audible. This audible changes the play to create an advantage for the offense. How about the defense, are they communicating with each other? Yes, they are communicating with gusto! The linebackers are yelling out the keys for the defensive alignment and they too will call a change of alignment at the line of scrimmage based upon the offensive alignment. And, the defensive backs are calling and changing defensive coverages based upon what the offense does when they come out of the huddle. Notice that both the offensive and defensive teams are engaged in a constant battle of correct alignment, both attempting to get an advantage over the other before the ball is snapped and the play begins.

In the world of selling a similar activity is going on each time a sales person meets or calls a customer. The customer is usually involved in some tactic to control the time together. They control by asking you to "Tell me what you can do for me?" "I'm very happy with who I'm buying from now?" or the classic "How much is it? Sounds high to me! I can get it cheaper from someone else." And then the sales person engages in objection handling, going into a "features and benefits" pitch, or uses a trial close to see if they are going to be lucky today.

Sales today involves more than some canned presentation that tells the customer or prospect all about you, your company and the product or service you are offering. It is more important to engage your customer in a business discussion that sounds more like a friendly conversation between equals. The best sales people are mastering customer involvement using the fine art of questioning.

The Questioning Model

Questioning is not easy, or everyone would be using this key tactic in their daily selling style. Questioning is an art that one must learn to master over a period of time. However, you can learn some basics of questioning and begin to practice your techniques on your peers.

Let's start by learning what types of questions to ask and the advantages of each type. First, the *detailed type* question is the most used question, especially by inexperienced sales people. These questions are designed to inform the sales person about specific details about the customer's situation. While there is usually some critical information to be learned in this group of questions, it is important to limit this type of questioning with the dominant decision maker. Why? Because the sales person is the only person benefiting from the answer! Imagine how many times a day or week this key person gets asked the same question by inexperienced sales people. This is the reason it has become very difficult to get to a key decision maker. The sales people have turned off the key buyer or decision maker to wanting another visit from a "sales person." Therefore, the sales person must find ways to discover the information needed from different sources. Key details need to be documented; yet alternative sources need to be identified. Alternatives could include doing basic research on the Internet using Google, MSN, Yahoo, Hoover's business reports, or other search engines. These search engines can provide you with articles on the company, profiles on the history of the company, locations of plants or headquarters, a list of key competitors and various financial news items. Another key source for basic information is the website of the company. Often you will find a list of officers or contacts, product listings and descriptions, and a list of locations, plants and subsidiaries.

This type of information, and this type of preparation, allows you to ask a different kind of question or statement. An example of this "smarter" question would be " I understand that you have six plants currently, is that correct? Or has this

---

Detailed Questions

» *What is your revenue?*
» *How many branches/plants/divisions do you have?*
» *Who are your currently buying "x" from?*
» *How long have you been with the company?*
» *How many people work here?*

---

changed recently?" This type of question or *statement-question* shows the customer that you have done some homework. They begin to place you into a different mental folder in their mind so you are beginning to reposition their perception of a sales person.

Now you move on to questions that uncover dissatisfactions in the current state of their area of the company – do this only after you ask permission to move to the next level of questions. Most sales people move into using probing questions to uncover problems like a prosecuting attorney. Rapidly firing off questions is not the appropriate tactic to use. This method of questioning is not the way to win friends and influence others in the business community. Always ask permission before digging into their minds. Getting approval first sets the stage for a more positive and helpful experience for both of you. How do you ask for permission? Simple. You only

Statement Questions

» *I understand that you have six plants in the mid west, is that correct?*

» *Your production lines are using brand 'y' machinery?*

» *My research shows that this plant produces approximately 1 million widgets per quarter - is that accurate?*

have to say something like "Do you mind if I ask you some questions?" If they ask you why you want to ask any questions, you respond by saying "Because it helps me understand your situation better, so we can learn if there is a business fit for our companies." This is a simple statement of reason. "Please allow me the time to learn about your situation so we can determine together if there is reason for us to do business together." This is a superior method, instead of going into a product demo and telling the customer all about the product or service, and hoping that the customer will discover a reason to buy from you. When using a product presentation, most sales people have no clue as to why the customer should buy from them!

So, the customer has given us permission to ask questions - what do we do now? Detail questions are not appropriate at this moment. So we need to use questions that will benefit both the sales person and the customer. Use *problem based questions* to uncover issues the customer may be having at that moment. Problem based questions are designed to uncover problems, concerns, issues and dissatisfactions in the current business environment. These questions get the customer thinking about their condition and the circumstances that are causing these issues.

Problem Based Questions

» *What areas of the supply chain would you improve if you could do it today?*

» *How many people are affected by a late delivery?*

» *What are your top three concerns regarding your production line / quality process suppliers / maintenance / inventory / etc...? (pick one)*

» *Are there any issues you have concerning _____ that you would like to share with me?*

» *How has productivity changed due to new machine operators?*

It is important to know that a customer that is satisfied with the current events will not be thinking about change or buying anything that may change the good thing they have currently. This is the reason for asking tough, attention getting questions. The tougher the question, the more the customer has to focus upon the question to give you the answer. In today's business world, nobody has enough time; therefore, they are thinking about any number of things when you are meeting together. Focus is difficult even in the best of times, but if you throw in a couple of project deadlines, this morning's new crisis, and the important committee meeting coming up in the next couple of hours… gaining their focus is critical to your success. The more focused and specific your questions are, the more thought and focus will go into the answer. The customer benefits from their answer due to the clarity of their own thought process. Sometimes a customer is surprised by their own answer as they realize they have a problem. Thus, it is harder for them to remain in a satisfied state. Curiosity enters the field of play and you now have the focused attention of the customer.

One of the most common errors made by sales people is that once the customer indicates that they have a possible problem, the sales person launches into a sales presentation with the old "features and benefits" pitch. Learn patience like the offensive team as they wait for the ball to be snapped. Remember, a presentation before other things have happened is like an illegal procedure penalty and you will lose yardage with your customer.

So what do you do next if you can't go into a sales presentation? You ask questions about the *effects* of the problem. You want to uncover the consequences of the pain, dissatisfaction or difficulty that they are currently facing.

Why should you have the customer uncover the effects or consequences? Because, they are involved in the discovery, and then their commitment to a solution becomes greater as the reality of the problem(s) becomes larger. The effects of the problem are quantified by the customer and will assist you in developing a return on investment. Since the customer is discussing the issues and their effects on their area

---

Effects Questions

» *What is the payroll cost per hour when a production line is shut down due to late delivery of inventory?*
» *When you have turnover of key machine operators - what does it cost you to train new operators?*
» *What does a reduction in productivity cost you?*
» *If your inventory has a quality issue - what does it cost you in terms of (network, customer satisfaction, overtime, shipping and supply chain, accounting, billing issues? (pick one)*

of responsibility, these questions are used to uncover other areas that are impacted by the issues and could cause other issues within the company. This escalation of the problem to areas outside the customer's direct area of influence can place the customer at risk if others find out. Therefore, the sense of urgency is increased to take action and solve the issue – sooner rather than later. Yet, the excellent sales person is still not through asking questions. If the buyer is beginning to ask about a solution, we need to learn what are the specific benefits of a solution to this buyer.

The *benefit questions* are now the focus of your questioning tactics. You are looking to learn how the buyer will benefit and what are the specific and quantifiable payoffs they will receive from a solution to their issues. Once they have provided this information, you will be able to accurately state the specific return on investment they will receive and there will be no debate. Why? Because they were involved in the determination of the numbers. They identified the pain and what it is costing the company at the moment. Then they identified and verified the returns and specific benefits to the solution that you offered.

The interesting thing about using the questioning model of selling, rather than a presentation model of selling, is that the customer usually sells themselves during the process and the closing is very simple. Usually, the only technique in closing is the invitation to start working together. A simple invitation to start and the answer is yes. Sometimes the customer will ask you the closing question due to higher sense of urgency for action. This is the time that selling is really a fun sport!

Learning the Decision Making Process

The second area of engagement with customers involves the use of some simple tactics to learn the specific decision making process that any buyer will use. Based upon questioning techniques, you can learn the specifics of how your customer will buy, and you will be able to tailor your offering to match the way they want to purchase. The interesting thing about these tactics is that the information has been available for over twenty-five years; yet, few sales people are even aware of this process. The sales people who have learned it are creating a competitive advantage over their competition. Why? The first reason is that the people using these methods create excellent rapport with their customers. The second reason is the sales person only asks the customer to buy when they are convinced it is time to ask, and the offer is made in the format that is easy for the customer to make a favorable decision.

There is no magic dust or miracle pill for this process. The major skill is listening to the customer, so you can learn the keys to the decision making door. Learning how your customer makes decisions is similar to the football team reading the stances and positioning of players in front of them on any play. Little signs like the knuckles turning white on the hand on the ground, which direction someone is looking as they come out of the huddle, or whom are they watching before the ball is put into play. These little signs, and several others, allow a defense to know before the play begins whether it is a running play or a passing play. If it is a running play, is the guard going to pull out and go to the other side to block someone? Or an offense will see little clues coming from a corner back that determines whether the pass defense is playing in a zone or man-to-man package. These signs are usually available to the players, if they know what to look for and how to execute based upon the signs they are getting.

In the world of selling, there are several areas where you can learn the best way to communicate with your customer. One of the simplest methods is to ask *"For you, what is important about product or service X?"* This simple question will get the buyer talking about the specifics of the buying criteria. In other words, using this simple question coupled with a couple of *"Is there anything else? "What else is important?"* then, you will learn exactly what will be evaluated during the decision making process. You can also learn if the customer has a very limited list of criteria (tough standards) or wants the world for little investment. Using this information you can determine if you have the right product or service, or if you will need to educate the buyer on the priorities for buying.

An interesting piece of information about your customer is whether they are goal oriented or more of a problem-solver. The reason this is important, relates to application, and to a sales person's discussions or presentations. If the customer is a problem-solver, then they need to hear about how you solve problems, not how you will get them to some goal that, frankly, they don't believe is as important as solving problems. Now for most sales people this is a difficult concept to learn because most sales people are goal oriented and they believe in the power of and the need for goals. Yet, customers can have a specific orientation to one or the other, and the sales person is responsible for communicating the message in the terms the customer can understand.

Another area that can challenge sales people is whether the customer is internally or externally motivated. In other words, if a customer is internally motivated, then they (and they alone) will make the decision. If a sales person tries to influence this person by using several testimonials and makes the mistake of strongly recommending an action, this customer is inclined to say "No". The only thing that matters to the internally driven person is how they feel about something and then they will be the judge and jury for the decision. On the other hand, the externally motivated buyer needs to know how others feel about the product or service, how others will react to any decision they make, and they want to know what you recommend as the best choice. Then they will go ask others in the company about their thoughts. With too many conflicts or choices, the externally motivated buyer shuts down. You will get a "No" and the more deadly 'stall' tactic!

One of my favorite communication challenges is identifying how a potential buyer knows when they will be convinced, and if now is time for the closing question. There are four possible tactics to follow depending upon how a customer answers the simple question *"How many times do they have to demonstrate a solution before you are convinced?"* One response shows the buyer is trusting of the seller and is immediately convinced that you are good and they are ready to buy. A second response shows that the buyer is never satisfied and you must convince them every time you present a solution. They want proof every time and are difficult to deal with every time. The third response will indicate that it takes a specific number of things – a number of visits, a number of testimonials, a number of referrals, a number of pilots to work properly, etc. Once you know the number of things necessary for the buyer to be convinced, you do not ask for the close until after the appropriate number has been reached; then you are positioned to ask for the business. The final response shows a time line that must be reached before any decision will be made to buy. I have seen buyers that operate on just a couple of days to a full year before they are convinced that you have the right solution. Any attempts to close before the magical time line is reached is an exercise of disappointment.

Other areas that need to be uncovered include the way the buyer processes information. There are two methods used. One is general or big picture processing of information. These people want the 30,000 ft. view of what will be working and what it will mean to the buyer. The other processor is the specific or detailed person. These people want all the information they can get their hands on for processing. They place all the details together to get to the big picture, yet if you start with the big picture – they are asking questions about potential details, so give the detailed version and they will be happy campers. If you have no details for the specific processor, then expect no deal. Simple. You can uncover the processor type by asking a simple question like *"Tell me about one of your favorite purchasing situations."* Then listen to the flow of the answer – general and conceptual, or specific and detailed?

The Basics of the Communication Process

The communication process is the most misunderstood or ignored basic process we use daily. Why is it misunderstood or ignored? Because the approach used by most people in delivering their communication messages is considered lazy language. People make statements like "That's just the way I am" or "I tell it the way it is!" or "That's the way I've always done it and I'm not going to change!" These are lazy people who are not interested in making "effective communication" their goal. In the engagement sport of customer contact, it is our responsibility to deliver the messages in the form and format that the customer will understand. Think effective relative to understanding the message.

The basic communication process is believed to have a sender – a message – and a receiver of the message. It is then believed that the receiver will be able to understand the meaning of the message just because the message was sent. This is a gross mistake on the part of the senders of messages.

Communication Process

This is similar to the situations that football players have when they move from high school to a top college program. Other than the pure pace and speed of the college game, the next biggest obstacle for high school players is to learn the offensive and defensive systems that are in place. If the coaches deliver terminology and assignments without any additional modifications or additions to their communication, the new players are lost. This is the major reason that very athletic and talented players get red shirted their freshman year, so they can learn the new systems and the terminology that is used. When a new player does not understand the system, they do not play or execute the plays very well and are ineffective.

The communication process has a message that is really neutral if you look only at the content or intent of the message. However, in the real world, the sender encodes the message with all the personal "stuff" which includes their value system, experiences, cultural issues, biases, prejudices, goals and objectives, as well as expectation and behavioral style. Behavioral style factors will create about 80% of communication issues. Learning about our own traits as the sender enhances effectiveness, because then we can understand the encoding side. Yes, that's only one aspect, and it directs us to another issue. The issue is now the receiver. They have a decoder process that takes the message through their personal filter system. This can confuse the message even more as the receiver's filters will limit some information, block key information, or totally misread the intent of the message. When you combine the encoding and decoding processes, it seems a miracle that we can get any communication of messages done effectively!

Remember the statement that about 80% of the issues causing communication conflict is based in behavioral style differences? You can learn about your behavioral style using simple assessments that will pinpoint your personal behavioral style. These assessments focus on your behavioral style factors or how you prefer to communicate with others. These assessments can accurately describe how you like to be communicated to, and how you do not like to be communicated to by others. This practice allows you to become aware of your tendencies regarding the pace you work and the priorities you place on yourself and others.

The next thing is to learn about all the other predominant behavioral styles and how to recognize the style of different customers. Why is this important? You will want to communicate with others using the behavioral style they possess. This practice is called flexing your style to others for effective communication.

The best football coaches have learned about assessments and are using them to get a better understanding of the communication differences of each player. Jimmy Johnson (the great coach of the Oklahoma State Cowboys, the Miami Hurricanes, and later the Dallas Cowboys of the NFL) used assessments to learn the natural strengths and weaknesses of each player on his team. He used this understanding to communicate and motivate each player according to the player's unique needs. Did it work? Well, he led his teams to conference championships, National championships and Super Bowl titles. There must be some truth to the technique.

There are opportunities to learn this information easily and become a better communicator overnight. Sales people from all parts of the country have told us how much this information has improved their positive communication with their customers and prospects. They gain rapport faster and develop trust at a faster pace using a more effective communication process based upon knowing the importance of behavioral style. The best sales people internalize behavioral style knowledge and find themselves naturally flexing to the style of the buyers during the sales process. And, they enjoy knowing more about themselves, knowing that flexing is only short term and is a stress-less activity. Most importantly, it allows them to be more productive in their daily sales results. Make a personal commitment to do a style assessment and get some feedback on how to use this information. It will make a big difference in your personal and professional life.

In summary, selling is a contact sport. Sales people can only be successful when they are successfully engaging customers. Being successful can be made simple by learning some simple techniques. The first of these techniques is the fine art of questioning. Questioning is a critical competence for the twenty-first century sales person and it is becoming more important in the management office! The second technique is to learn how to identify the customer's buying process and sell to your customer the way they want to buy. Too often sales people are selling the way they would buy, rather than the way the customer wants to buy – major mistake! Learn the techniques that place you in the winner's circle more often.

Finally, learn your base style of communication and how you do the things you do. Self-awareness is one of the four horsemen from part one, so learn about you. Then you can learn about the other behavioral style traits as well as how to recognize the behavioral style traits in others. Then learning to flex your behavioral style to insure the effectiveness of your communication becomes an improvement goal and will lead to increased opportunities and more success. More successful contact with people can make a difference in your results.

Coach Voss's Chalk Talk

Chapter Five: Actively Engaging Others

- » *Selling is a contact sport - learn to be effective.*
- » *Questioning is more effective than telling.*
- » *Proper technique is critical in the questioning process.*
- » *Use questions and listen.*
- » *Watch for signs the customer gives you to know how they will make a decision to buy.*
- » *You must learn how your customers process information.*
- » *Deliver offers and statements the way the customer processes information rather than your way.*
- » *Sell to customers - the way they want to buy.*
- » *Knowing your behavioral style provides you with awareness of your natural strengths and weaknesses.*
- » *Flexibility of style is a winning attribute.*

Chapter Six

Practicing to Improve Results

Winning football teams just don't show up for the games and expect to win. They practice continually to get to the next level. In the spring, they work on the fundamentals and the basics. In the summer, they come together to begin the process of learning their plays, the systems, and the reads; also, they practice the execution of plays and formations until the players don't have to think about the variables. They have internalized the knowledge and now they just execute their assignments with consistency and effectiveness.

So why is it that sales people tend to only show up for their games? What is their reasoning for feeling that they can be successful by just "winging-it" when in the presence of customers? This is one of the big questions in the world of selling. Why don't sales people practice more?

In this chapter, we will explore the importance of practice and personal improvement using practice time. We will also explore a couple of the most effective techniques for learning and internalizing the best practices for selling. Like the great teams, sales people can learn to practice and train for improving their results and moving to the top of their field and then the hard part... staying at the top every year. The key is to stay active in your learning and stay ahead of the thundering herd of average sales people. Make a commitment to be a winner and read on through this chapter.

Continuous Improvement – the Kaizen Process

When you are an intense fan of college football, you will follow the development of players from the time they enter as freshmen to the last game of their college eligibility. Watching a player improve each year is a true pleasure. The winning programs are designed to get good talent in the program and allow them to develop through good coaching and individual drive to get better each year. Football players will get faster, stronger and smarter as they progress during their tenure. Occasionally, we will see a player that does not improve. Why don't they improve? Usually that player has a couple of issues. The most common is an attitude problem. They believe they are already good enough, and lose focus on the fact that everyone around them is getting bigger, faster and smarter. The other major issue occurs when the player does not take personal responsibility for his own development. Here we find that the player does not get involved in the off-season or voluntary development process. They assume that the only thing they have to do is to show up at practice, practice the plays, and then they will play in the games. In other words, it becomes the coaches' responsibility to get the player ready to play on game day. This is a very unfortunate situation, as the player does not reach his full potential. People discuss this player in terms like "He shoulda, coulda, and woulda been great!" followed by a statement like "Wonder where he is today?"

Sales people need to be aware that the sales manager and training department are not responsible for their ultimate development. The top sales people take an attitude of continuous learning and development. This leads to taking personal responsibility for learning to be the best in their profession. In fact, our experience in working with sales teams finds the top people are always the first in line for a developmental opportunity. Often they fund the development process from their own paychecks.

Becoming a lifetime learner is the key to being employable for a lifetime. This is very different from being employed for life in today's corporate environment of reorganizations, mergers, restructures and even company failures and closings. Some of the people that expect the company to take care of them because of their tenure make a very poor assumption. Top performers take control of their progress by setting a goal of continuous learning. It is amazing what can be learned from seminars, books, and articles on the sales profession and specific industries. We often hear self-learners state "It's amazing that I've been successful based upon what I didn't know last week, last month or last year."

Some sales people ask why do they need to learn when there is nothing new to learn? First, these people are in denial about learning and information. The information age is accelerating the discovery of new things to learn. In fact, the experts are reporting that general knowledge is doubling every three years. Assuming this to be true, it is then possible that one third of a person's knowledge will become obsolete or incomplete by the end of the year! This means we have to continuously learn to maintain our current knowledge base. Learning does not guarantee getting ahead of the knowledge curve. Focused learning in specific areas will increase the probability of getting ahead of the knowledge curve in the sales profession. However, doing nothing or very little in the areas of learning and development will place a person well behind the knowledge curve. When companies begin looking at reducing head count in the sales organization, the non-learners are at risk of losing their job. Increase your abilities and knowledge to avoid warming the bench in times of critical needs or crisis.

One insight that has been pointed out from people who excel at their personal continuous improvement process is that when they are actively learning an interesting thing happens - they discover more "secrets" to success. Their natural curiosity increases as they are exposed to more information, and they move into the world of the unknown! Yet, as they study the information or processes, they realize it has been there for a long time – they were just unaware of this knowledge. The addition of knowledge and the ensuing application of this knowledge improve their productivity and performance results. We're back to the old "Law of Cause and Effect." Change the causes and you will get different results.

Application Exercise

When a football team installs a new offensive play, they don't wait until game day to execute it for the first time. They practice the play first. In fact, they practice it over and over again until they have achieved total memory of how to do it right. This allows for explicit learning and application of the fundamentals of the play so that the execution during a game will be more successful.

In the world of selling, unlike football, salespeople have the opportunity to practice plays before ever getting in front of the customer. Role Playing has been available to sales teams for decades. Since role playing is against the most knowledgeable and hardest critics – our peers – there has been a tendency to avoid this excellent tool for learning. The ability to adjust and perfect our selling techniques using this old method is priceless and can be used in meetings, on the phone, while driving to a customer site, and with formal developmental processes. However, many sales people tend to dislike this tool. Frankly, when they hear the term "role play" some actually get sick and leave.

Therefore, a new term has emerged to replace role play. It is the "application exercise". When you are learning something new, the best practice is application of the new information in a simulation of real time situations.

Application exercises allow the sales person to practice a new technique or method before they are in front of a real customer. This practice allows the sales person to get active feedback relative to their performance. Suggestions and helpful hints can be provided on the spot for performance improvement. Experts in adult learning have found that the immediacy of feedback is a key factor in higher levels of retention in new learning. Since people tend to remember what they did wrong in situations, the use of immediate feedback will allow the sales person to remember or even internalize a new concept after the first practice session.

Learn to use the application exercise for such examples as:

1.   *New product rollouts,*
2.   *Special promotions,*
3.   *Learning new rapport building techniques,*
4.   *Learning to flex to the different behavior styles you will meet,*
5.   *And any other new processes.*

Our experience with sales people is that they need to actually do the new process in a practice environment, or they will not attempt it in an actual customer meeting using old comfortable methods with no positive results. Having knowledge available and not using it at the appropriate time is the same as not knowing it in the first place!

To be like the great football players, you need a personal developmental process that you work in every year and all year. Success does not come as a natural event for most of us. We are responsible for developing our winning edge. While working with industry superstars in selling, we have found that they are not two, three, five, or ten times better people. They just stay focused and execute on the little things all the time. Their results, interestingly enough, are often two, three, five or ten times greater than the average sales person. Be a winner, practice your skills and become a real professional.

Using Video and Audio Techniques

One of the things that makes the best teams better is the amount of time they review game and practice videos. The coaches use the video review principles to remove any doubt regarding the evaluation of practice sessions or game time performance. The video shows the real story to the player and the coach.

Like role play, the video camera does not see much time in the halls of sales groups. Why not? There appears to be many different reasons, yet the common theme is that sales groups just don't want to, or there is some unknown fear factor that causes very outgoing people to become very shy. Again, this is an unfortunate reaction. The sales teams that have used the video process as a tool to improve their performance have learned to overcome deficiencies uncovered in the early videos and they see immediate improvement. Most of the time, the sales person's self-esteem and self-confidence increases on the spot. This leads to higher levels of performance results within days and weeks rather than months and years.

The practice of video taping presentations or mock customer interactions is like role play on steroids! Why? The individual also gets to see him- or herself in action like everyone else. In some cases, this is the first time they have seen themselves perform a sales activity. The learning is instant and very memorable. Sales people tell us, years after the initial video sessions, about the positive impact it had on both their confidence and performance. The reason for this is simple. When people see themselves improving, their performance in presentations, questioning methods, gaining rapport or any other sales related practice, the application moves from positive thinking to positive knowing. As a sales person I may think I'm good now. When I see myself perform at a high level, I now know that I can do it and do it well. This drives an increase in confidence, and provides a new feeling of reinforced self-efficacy or mastery of the sales skills, thus becoming a self-fulfilling prophecy in performance. When people are willing to take action regarding their personal development, ultimately the results come in multiples.

Another tool that can be used by a sales person is the audio tape or digital recorder. This small handheld device can be used to practice a presentation as you are traveling to work or to a customer's office. This tool is especially useful for capturing new ideas or creative ways to solve a customer's issues. It has also been used to learn about your speech habits and patterns. You can practice where to place emphasis in pointing out information to customers. Since most sales people have a tendency to "wing-it" with customers, this could be the planning tool of choice when used to capture those winging thoughts!

Some sales people have used tape recorders to learn how to control pace and tempo for presentations or how to deal with customers with a very different style than the sales person. Again, practice when used as a development tool rather than punishment or a negative tool, will have immediate and positive results for both the sales person and his or her company.

The key for any improvement process is the active use of the tools and techniques for evaluating the level of performance. Having tools and not using them is as bad as being able to read and choosing not to read. This is a clear sign of impending stupidity. Become a winner and practice your trade using application exercises and video yourself for immediate review and improvement opportunities.

In summary, it is your responsibility to accept the role of developmental officer for your personal improvement process.

Learn what your natural strengths and weaknesses are by using assessments. Think about what traits are necessary for you to perform your job at excellent levels and compare to your assessment information. Develop a plan of action for improving the traits that are important to your job performance. Fine-tune your strengths and work on your weaknesses that impact your results.

Use application exercises to practice your techniques and learn how to improve these techniques using the immediacy of the feedback. Use the video camera to capture your performance. You can review the practice session and accelerate your learning. See yourself improve during retakes or after learning new techniques and applying them. Feel the difference in your self-confidence and self-esteem as you eliminate the uncertainty or ambiguity that existed when the video captured your performance.

Using audio tape or digital recorders to capture your voice, pace, tone, and behavior style gives you the opportunity to make choices and actively plan and practice your presentations. Go the extra mile in developing your skills and maintain that winner's edge for your lifetime. Be a winner and practice like a winner. Losers avoid practice time and are excellent at the negative emotion of denial – "_Didn't even know I am lying!_" Be responsible for your excellence. Take an active stance and launch your career to the next level of performance.

To reach the highest pinnacles of success, a salesperson must be prepared to use the proactive techniques covered in this chapter. Self-discipline and focus combined with continuous improvement will separate you from the average player. Follow the old slogan – "No pain, no gain." Practice will create some initial pain, yet the results of your gains will move you into the "playmaker" status. To borrow a quote from an old pro coach - "Perfect practice leads to perfect plays". Make a personal decision to unlock "all" your hidden talents.

Coach Voss's Chalk Talk

Chapter Six: Practice

» *Continuous improvement is a personal choice and responsibility.*

» *Losers "wing-it" while winners have a plan for improvement - and follow the plan.*

» *Role plays and "Application exercises" allow you to learn to do things the right way without real penalties.*

» *No Pain, No Gain - swallow your pride and practice with feedback.*

» *Use videos for awareness and faster personal improvement.*

» *Use self-discipline and focus to separate from the average performers.*

» *Remember this quote: "Perfect practice leads to perfect execution."*

Game Three

The Selling Game

Introduction

*Where Strategic Thinking +
Tactical Techniques = SUCCESS*

Part three covers the game of selling, where we show how sales strategy coupled with tactical techniques equal sales success. Success for today's sales person will depend upon his or her ability to marry strategy and tactics. In years past, a salesperson could learn a presentation, call a customer, get an appointment with a decision maker, deliver the presentation, and expect to get an answer regarding the sale. Today, the field of play has changed. The salesperson needs to understand the actual application of their product or service, discover whom to call, meet with multiple buying influencers, gain rapport with everyone, build a respect and trust based relationships, show that they have successfully dealt with the customer's issues, and then they have to defend their position against aggressive and capable competitors.

In this section, we will explore the games of selling that the sales person needs to be prepared to deal with in order to excel in their profession. The first of the selling games is to master the Game Plan. The days of "winging it" with customers are gone. Yes, it is important to be flexible and adaptive to unique situations; however, a game plan will prepare the sales person for expected contingencies. Like a good football team, the sales person needs to have both an offensive and defensive game plan. This allows for excellent execution that both creates and delivers consistent results.

The next game within the selling game is how you manage your Game Clock. Few teams are successful when they do not pay attention to the game clock. In fact, one of the most common penalties in football is the delay of game penalty. While on the surface it is only a minor infraction, it often loses either the team's forward momentum or, on occasion, the game. The most common effect is that the team has to double its efforts just to get back to where they were! How often has a sales person failed to manage his game clock with a critical customer or prospect? Lack of time management is one of the major causes of failure within the sales profession.

The next game within the sales game is making Half-Time Adjustments. The best-coached teams have a reputation of making accurate half-time adjustments based upon what they learned during the first half. Often we see salespeople continue down the same path with customers without any idea or discovery that the strategy is not working, or that their competition is working a better plan. Without adjustments to your plans and actions, you could be doing the wrong things very well. One example that often we see, is the sales person continuing to call on the wrong person within a customer's company, thus leading to building terrific rapport and trust with someone that can not and will not make a buying decision. What a waste of effort and time when the only thing that sales people have to trade is their precious time.

Another game within the selling game is the art of managing the Game Officials. While coaches and captains will set up the game officials during the course of the game to get the close calls in the end of the game, sales people need to make certain that they are calling on the right officials for their sales process to win. Sales people that just call on a particular title are not seeking out the true decision makers for their specific selling situation. Often there is more than one influencer - some dominant and some negative, some that actually want you to win and then others that have a different idea of who should win the contract. It is your job to recognize and work the right officials to get those favorable calls at the critical points in the game or the sales cycle.

The final game within the selling game is the Two-Minute Drill. The interesting point about the two-minute drill is it prepares you to maintain a win, or to pull out a win at the last moment. The better teams are coached on situational two-minute drills and are prepared to deal with issues in a proactive way. Losing teams tend to give up if they are behind or just begin to draw plays in the dirt, believing that their probability for success is closer to zero. Sales people need to understand that if you are winning, it is time to shorten the clock and get closure, which is a sense of urgency for completion without taking any unnecessary risks. If you are losing, it's time to take a risk to change the outcome. The key point within the two-minute drill is to remember to play to win at all times. Losers play NOT to lose and surprise – they end up losing! Eliminate the "prevent defense" unless you have a signed contract.

Chapter Seven

Game Plans

Winning football teams have winning game plans. The game plan will include an overall strategy for winning the game against specific competition. It is important to note that the best teams change their game plans depending upon their competition's strengths and weaknesses. And seldom do these teams use the same game plan for every game. They do have a playbook with all available offensive and defensive plays that the team could use. Yet, it is important to change up the order or progression of the plays called, -strategy- or the opponent can anticipate your actions. Your overall plan is a strategy that if executed well will offset the other team's competitive advantage.

While the game plan has an overall strategy, the plan is further divided into offensive and defensive game plans. Each unit will practice their specific plan against the anticipated tactics of their opponent. This practice time will insure the proper execution on game day.

Sales people need to adopt this practice if they truly

want to be excellent in their profession. An overall strategy is important in creating a mental model of how the sales person expects to win the customer's decision.

The first mission for the sales person is to create a mental model of the ideal customer. This simple exercise is not easy, since it forces the sales person to make critical choices about the customers he or she wants to find and develop. This process is similar to an architect creating a vision of a building that they want to build and describing all the parts and pieces that will go into the construction of the building. While a sales person is not building a building, they are building a "book of business." A sales person can create their entire list of customers based upon the type of customers that they want to have. What traits does your ideal customer profile possess? See Appendix for Ideal Customer worksheet.

If you have an existing customer base, the simplest method is to create a chart that will help you focus on the ideal. First, create a column that lists your best customers. In the next column list the traits and characteristics that make them your best customers. Skip the next column and go to the fifth column and list your worst customers both current and past. Go to the fourth column and list the characteristics and traits of these customers. Reflect on your work and make any additions or subtractions in the columns. Now the time has come for some serious decision-making. Using the center column, outline the traits and characteristics that you would prefer your customers possessed. This outline would contain the primary descriptors of what an ideal customer would look, sound, and feel like to work with. Using this profile, you would then use it as a screening tool against all leads and suspects. There are some companies that hold their sales people to very high standards and will reject potential customers from the "sales funnel" if they do not match the ideal customer profile. While this appears to be more of an exception than the rule with sales companies, it can change the quality of your customer base as well as impact the results of the sales team.

If you are new to sales and there is no published ideal customer profile, then spend some time talking with the sales manager and the top sales people in your group, and visit the marketing group. The idea is to ask questions of these key people about the existing customer base. You want to get their descriptions of the best and worst customers and what factors did they use in making their choices. This information will give you the basis for making a profile of your own. Taking the time to develop this profile will save you from heartache down the road when you find some of the "worst customer" accounts. One of the traits of the superstar is knowledge of when to walk from a customer that will not match up to the unique strengths of your company.

We have worked with sales people that made the decision to identify their ideal customer profile and then work the profile accordingly. When the company or sales person is diligent in following their paths to their ideal customers, the results have been outstanding. Both sales revenue AND profitability increases, rather than the usual outcome of sales OR profitable growth from building a customer base.

The Offensive Plan

Now that you have the overall strategy and the ideal customer profile, you are ready to develop offensive game plans. The interesting thing about good football programs is that they limit the number of plays that are practiced during the game week to the plays that have been selected for the game plan. Why? Because of the limited amount of time they have for practice. This is the same situation you will face. There is only so much time during the week that can be used to plan. The majority of your time should be used in customer interaction, either by phone or face to face. This is the time that truly counts for the sales person. However, if you feel that it is okay to just show up at a customer's office and "wing-it" until you feel good about the visit, well, you will miss the major reason for being at the customer's office. By just showing up without an appointment you will position yourself as unprofessional. You will also show the customer that your time is not very valuable since you are willing to just hang around in the lobby until your contact is available! Set a plan and work your plan.

Okay, we have determined that you need an offensive game plan, so what do you need to plan? There are three primary offensive plans to develop. The first plan is the Account Plan. This plan consists of your most important existing accounts, usually major accounts and potential targeted accounts. A targeted account is a potential customer that fits the ideal customer profile. The objective of the targeted account or major account is to identify product or service strategies that will maximize the relationship with the customer. It looks at factors such as total potential business with this customer, how much do you have now, the percentage of account share, and what areas of the company can you target a campaign to penetrate or expand your business? The key to this account research is to determine current business and desired levels of business, examine the gaps (if any), and determine the strategy you could use to close the gap. This plan is usually an annual plan that can be reviewed on a quarterly basis to determine the progress being made on the plan.

One of the things that you can do to improve your Account Plan activities is to look at the areas your customers have in common. Then examine what and how the customers are using your products or services. Here you are looking for strategies or applications that you have not used on certain accounts that could be used to increase account share. Then, look at different industry types by using a best practices thinking approach. You can find patterns that you could promote to an existing customer or prospect that could open the door to increased business. The major objective of the Account Plan is to take time to think about your accounts and prospects. Focus your thinking on how you could increase your business while the customer significantly improves their situation. This is important since the faster the customer sees how they can improve their situation with limited risk, the faster they will be calling you to take action.

The next plan for the sales person is the Opportunity Plan. This a monthly plan where the sales person lists the identified sales opportunities. During the month either the sales person has targeted a possible sales promotion, or the customer has concurred that they have a specific need. Then the sales person can calculate the possible upcoming sale. This can be identified as a single sales objective or a targeted sales goal. The key is to be specific in the sales goal. It is important to be specific so you can plan the calls properly and identify the right group of influencers for the success of the sales process. It is important to understand that in the larger organizations that you are selling to, they can have the decision makers and influencers at various levels within the company. And you can have multiple sales goals within the same company while having totally different buying groups. This is one of the reasons for the Opportunity Plans so you can determine who, what and when decisions are to be made within the customer's organization. The old days of having one decision maker for all decisions is limited only to very small companies with an autocratic leader who makes all the decisions. Develop a game plan for your identified opportunities to improve your success rates.

Finally there is the last form of planning that is the most overlooked and that should be the most used. It is the Call Plan. Why is it the most overlooked considering the potential number of Call Plans? It goes back to the behavioral style of the sales person. Most sales people have a natural desire to "wing it" while avoiding any form of written plan. This is very unfortunate due to the wasted time with a customer – which today is the most valuable time you have as a sales person. Your customer is too busy and has no extra time to waste on a poorly prepared sales person. This is the reason that so many sales people hold their present customer relationships on such high ground! These customers will actually take time to meet with the sales person and share valuable information. Yet, most sales people don't show their customer that they value this time together by using an agenda and having a plan with specific questions to uncover needs or consequences of issues that if left unchanged will cost the customer – either personally or departmentally. This process shows the customer that you care about their results and your job is to assist them in identifying areas to improve. What a difference this attitude makes on your business relationships.

Defensive Game Plans

Your defensive game plan includes three specific areas. The first is to research your customer. Just like a football team will break down their opponent's game films and read articles on both the Internet and the local sports pages, you need to examine and research your customers and potential or targeted accounts. While the football coaches and players are looking at film to determine the tendencies, strengths, and weaknesses of their opponents, you want to learn about the key players in your customer's organization. Find out what new managers have recently been added to the company and where did they come from. If a key person has recently been hired and they came from a company that exclusively used your major competitor – then you have some major planning to do. What are the chances that you could lose an existing account? What strategies do you need to focus upon to lock up the account during this transition? What accounts could you focus upon now if the higher probability is you will lose this account to our competitor? Could we now get the business from the key player's old company? You need to think of yourself as a natural researcher for untapped opportunities. They are present, but we cannot see them if we are looking down or in the other direction. Think all the time - what if? Just like a good football team that responds to an opponent's tactics and counters the tactics to stop or slow down their momentum, we can develop contingency plans by using common research methods and by staying alert.

An additional point in using research is to identify your

customer's major goals and objectives. A publicly owned company has to submit detailed financial information, which includes statements of direction and organizational focus to governmental entities. These are available to you in printed or online forms. It is difficult to read some of this information; yet, as you train yourself in its use you can prepare action plans that can make a difference for the customer. Another area to watch is business journals in the customer's cities as well as business sections for the local newspapers in the customer's cities. This information provides names of key people and can provide insight into strategies as well as any upcoming changes in the organizational structure.

The next area is called a DOS analysis. This is a variation of the old SWOT methods of examining an organization. The process involves identifying Dangers both to the account itself and your relationship with the account. You want to identify anything that could negatively impact the business in the near term. By identifying all potential dangers you can prioritize based upon the probability of this event actually happening. Then you would have time to develop a quick contingency plan if it were to happen. Again the key is to BE PREPARED.

The next step is to identify any potential Opportunities that the customer has to grow their business and grow your sales too. New plants, product expansions, new products, consolidation of several plants into the one that you service, favorable changes in key positions of influence, and acquisitions made by the company with groups that you are currently not doing any business are all examples of opportunities.

The final step of the DOS process is to identify the Strengths of the customer. Examples include their important relationships that could influence other customers for you, financial acumen and strength of the company, their market position within their industry, growth percentages, and the level of alignment between your customer and your company to insure continued success. If partnerships are important within the industry you sell to, have you been successful in developing boundary-less relationships. Meaning that it is very difficult to determine where the separation point is between your company and your client's.

By understanding the depth of the DOS process you can prepare contingency plans to offset dangers, to expand opportunities, and to utilize the natural strengths between both your company and your customer's organization. This is a win-win situation.

Competitor Matrix

To know the enemy is a key military strategy. Every sales person is responsible for understanding the strengths and weaknesses of their competition. One of the best methods for sales people is to create a competitor matrix. This matrix is a system that is designed to provide intelligence regarding who customers are using or who is going after your accounts.

The matrix is basically a spreadsheet with the competitors listed on one axis and a list of characteristics or traits on the other axis. Under each competitor identify the specific characteristics and traits that they possess or position with their actions and marketing. Identify their real strengths and weaknesses in each area (refer to Appendix for complete Competitor Matrix worksheet).

You can also have a general strategy line for each competitor.

This allows you to track information of how they are using it in the field to position themselves against your company and the other competitors. This is important because when you target a new customer, you must prepare for the strategy that will be used against you. If you know that Competitor A is a low price company and they position all their efforts on low price, you can prepare your questions for your key contacts to determine the true role that price will take in the decision process. If you learn that price is the most important thing for this customer, you can make a decision regarding how hard you plan to work this business or if you even want to spend that time working an account that matches up with your strengths? However, if you learn that price is not as important as three other factors (with which you have an advantage over Competitor A) then you know to focus your time on winning this account. Alignment is important between the desired features that a customer wants and expects to the natural strengths of your company.

The Dreaded RFP

Some sales people actually look forward to receiving a RFP, Request for Proposal, out of the blue. This would be like a coach of a Division I-A football powerhouse getting a call out of the blue from a Division II-A team saying "we want to play you next fall. Pay us $500,000 and we will come to your house and you will get a win, a bigger paycheck and a chance to play all your players in an actual game". At first, this looks appealing, however there are three negative issues:

  1.   The team's fans don't like playing low ranked

teams,

2. The NCAA limits the number of II-A opponent games that count as actual wins for bowl eligibility, and

3. The polls would penalize the team points in their rating system (human or computer).

This is the same thought process that you must use in dealing with RFP's that you get out of the blue. If it's too good to be true, then there is a catch to it. The position you want to take with an RFP, is to call the contact and tell them that it is your practice to meet with key personnel and learn about their issues and the specific problems. This is a key part, because if they are unwilling to meet with you, so that you can better serve their specific needs, then they already have the winner selected. You have become the mechanism that they will use to validate that their choice is quoting market compatible prices. Another way of looking at this is to look at the specifications within the RFP. You can usually determine who the competitor is for the specifications that match their products or services rather than yours. Always remember the old accountants' phrase "If you find your numbers on any column after the 'C' column, you are just column fodder for the selected seller!" Ouch, that hurts!

The key to your success, if you are selling to an industry that uses RFP's in a natural course of business, is to get into the account first and set the standards. If you are doing your job of engaging the different players in the account, asking the right type of questions, involving the customer in determining the course of action, and specifying your product or service's unique value proposition for the RFP, then you are in the

"B or C" column of spreadsheet and are positioned to win! PREPARE and PLAN for successful actions.

For the non-financial sales person, the columns used in this example refer to spreadsheets used to compare price quotes between suppliers. The A column has a history of being the favored or existing supplier and the B thru Z columns are used to ensure competitive or low pricing.

Coach Voss's Chalk Talk

Chapter Seven: Game Plans

» *Winner's have a game plan - loser's just show up and play.*

» *Offensive game plans show what is possible and are actively used by winners.*

» *Defensive game plans provide knowledge and insite into your customer's methods and tendencies.*

» *Prepare and Plan for successful actions.*

Chapter Eight

Managing the Game Clock

Winning football coaches watch how their team is managing the game clock.

This practice is not only limited to the end of the game, where most sales people begin to pay more attention to the clock, as in the end of the month or end of a quarter. The excellent teams realize that the actual game clock runs for a full sixty minutes, not thirty or only the last two minutes, and the full sixty minutes must be managed in order to win against excellent competition. If a team focuses on or competes only for fifty-five minutes, then they will usually get beat by a more focused and conditioned team in the last minutes of the game. There are critical games played every weekend during the college football season where a highly ranked team gets upset by another team simply because they lost focus and concentration.

There are three areas of clock management that we are going to discuss. The first factor is the **sense of urgency** developed by teams and sales people. The best football teams develop a high level of urgency to take the game from the opponent as soon as possible. Their goal is to establish a lead and take the other team out of their game plan and force the opponent into a predictable game of catching up. When the winning team maintains their focus and high concentration levels, they usually put the game in the "win column" early, and then more players get to experience the game and the team benefits from the added depth it creates.

Relating this concept to a sales team is easy. Sales managers have stated for decades, "They wish their sales people would show a sense of urgency and get into a customer's office!" This common theme shows that every one is getting on the sales field early and often. Managing the game clock is a simple matter of making critical choices with the use of one's time. Abraham Lincoln stated, *"Good things may come to those who wait, but only the things left by the people who hustle."*

Procrastination is the number one killer of great intentions. If you wait to make calls until the moon and the stars are in alignment, then someone else has already gotten in the door ahead of you. If they are in first, they can position the sales objective to align with their products and services, and then you will be playing the "catching up" game. Your competitor can anticipate your moves and position to offset any of your arguments or ideas.

The concept of hustle or sense of urgency can be a real asset to those sales people that understand "how to use it properly". The reason for the "use it properly" phrase is to remind you to have a plan first. A plan focuses you on managing the flow of the game. Wingers who rush into an account and start talking about their products and services and their company's history and reputation, remind me of the football teams that get all pumped up on pure emotion. They start off all fired up and do well until the first bad thing happens, and then there is no focus to stay the course of the game. Bad habits and poor decisions begin to show up during the course of the game and the outcome is that they come in second in a field of two! There is no purpose to guide the sales process for the *wingers*. Consistent winners use a game plan and follow the planned process to advance the probability of success on their terms. The key is to consistently stay in the game by working your high priority accounts on a daily basis, insuring that you are managing the game and the game clock.

When you are first into the account, you can set the expectations of what success will look like when the buying decision is made. Your goal is to develop a network of contacts that will keep you advised on any new projects or opportunities in the customer's business. This requires that you have a plan for making consistent contact with all the influencers in your accounts. How does this translate into managing the game clock? In the world of college football, it deals with the offense running the proper plays to burn the clock when they're ahead or conserving time when they are behind. In the world of sales, the sales person needs to follow-up immediately to customer questions, send notes after a visit or phone call, send a hand written thank you note for orders, return phone calls within a specific time frame (think less than one hour), send new information, reports, or white papers of interest to a contact within the account, and otherwise show that he or she cares about the customer with his or her actions. By having a sense of urgency with your customer contacts, you are developing a trust-based relationship. This allows you to develop a positive reputation with the customer, showing that you are dependable and will go the extra mile for them in the clutch.

So the key factors in having a sense of urgency include getting into the accounts before your competitors, managing the game tempo, and developing a trust-based relationship as a dependable person that they can count on when they need you. There is another concept that needs to be addressed for the successful clock management of the sales process.

When do you make contact with the key or dominant decision maker? The traditional sales person usually calls on the same people and at lower levels within the customer's account. This puts them in the commodity zone trap. A problem can occur when the traditional sales person gets a chance to meet someone at a higher level within the account. While on the surface this is not a bad thing, it becomes a bad thing if the sales person immediately goes into sales presentation mode. They will tell the decision maker all about their product or their service's features and benefits or all about the seller's company or worst themselves! This is like the emotionally fired up team – it's all about them! The more successful sales person would have researched the account and learned about their issues and challenges. Then when encountering the key decision maker, they are ready to discuss the account and the business reason to do business with the seller. Unfortunately, this is not the mainstream practice of sales people. If it was the mainstream, we would have fewer commodity traps, shorter sales cycles, higher margins and longer term account relationships.

Buying Cycles meet the Sales Process

The traditional sales person usually runs into an account, uncovers one issue, and launches into a sales presentation. This is similar to an offense that throws long passes on every play hoping for a touchdown. Now it is true that you can get lucky every once in a while and actually score! The problem then becomes how do you score again? The customer will usually change the rules on you so that will not happen again, particularly when they do not like their results.

The inner*active* sales person will understand that there are two processes in play with a customer. First, there is the sales process that is used by the sales person to win business. This process can be very complex or very simple depending upon the nature of the industry and what is being sold. It is very important for the sales person to know what their sales process is and the order of the steps involved. The order is important since if you skip several of the steps in the name of efficiency (a fool's sense of urgency), the sale process will unfold and become lost at the last minute because of the missing steps. Something or someone will bring up a critical issue and kill the deal or, worse, give the deal to the competition. The second process is the *customer's buying cycle*. The basic buying cycle includes a customer moving from satisfied in the current state, to being dissatisfied, then to the discovery of options, to an evaluation of the options, to the selection or decision to change, to a review of the expected results, and finally back to being either satisfied or dissatisfied. This process could take several days to several years, again depending upon the complexity of the purchase and the impact upon the organization.

The number one issue with sales people is that they have a tendency to launch their sales process without paying any attention to where the buyer is in their buying cycle. Sales people have gone through their entire sales process including discounting their price, before the buyer even enters the buying process! What a waste of time and effort on the part of the sales person. This is an example of poor clock management. By refusing to work a sales plan and align it with the buying cycle, the sales person has placed himself or herself in the position of having NO ROOM to negotiate when the customer finally gets to the point of making a decision. The result is a number two position in a two person game.

The wise sales person will check the buyer's position in their buying process before any expectations or commitments are made. The old rule of "no need, no sell" is still valid today. There is no reason to enter into a presentation or quote prices until you know more about the situation. What quarter is the customer currently playing in the game? Knowing this will enable you to make the necessary choices to enter the game using the proper strategy and tactics to position you for the win. Using the offensive unit all the time is a loser's game. Use game strategies that match up with "down and distance" issues and the game clock (down and distance refers to the down – 1st thru 4th – and the yardage necessary to reset the down to first down – thus giving the offensive team more opportunities to score points.). Adjustments and changes can be made before the end of the game; the issue is to manage your game to the winners' bracket.

Sales people have stated that sometimes they are so far behind it makes no difference what and how well they perform. This can be an actual truth; however, the key is how they manage the long-term clock. This point is directly related to the development of a winning program rather than just winning a game. It is important for sales people to step back and do an assessment of how their "program" is doing. Are they establishing a perennial top-five program or will they become a one-year wonder? The challenge is to create a mindset that you want to become a member of the elite group that wins every year. You want to play for the top honor every year. The key is to identify what you do really well and do it more often. Then find the areas that must improve if it impacts the ability to join the membership of the elite. Great football programs spend time reviewing game film, identifying what worked and what did not work, and they develop plans to eliminate the mistakes and improve on the things that will make a difference next season. This is the one thing that a sales person can count on to improve their results. Improve the critical success factors and focus on the future while you deliver results in present.

Increasing Probabilities of Success

In the world of college football, clock and game management is a necessary strategy for continuous success. It is also important to *identify priorities* before the season as well as during the game. An example, of before the season, could be that the coach after reviewing the past year's game film determines that several losses were due to an overall lack of strength and size in the defensive line. This led to other teams being able to push the defensive line around and gain yardage at critical points of the game, which usually means the other team is managing the clock and the game situation at a high level. Thus, a good coach will immediately place the returning lineman on a strength and conditioning program to improve their position and the coach will recruit bigger and stronger defensive lineman for the next year.

A sales person can have his or her sales manager observe him or her in the field and watch for areas for improvement. He or she could watch his or her own "application exercise" videos, or he or she could simply reflect on his or her successes and failures and determine his or her own productivity gaps. Once identified, he or she can set an improvement process into motion. Any serious improvement requires a plan of action and a review of the results. This includes tracking of activities and developing ratios for measuring improvement and results.

An interesting point in clock management is when to call a time out? In the heat of the game sometimes it is necessary to call a time out. This could be a critical point in the game whereby you need to discuss your strategy or tactic with someone else to get validation that it is correct. Or the situation makes it necessary to brainstorm with others about using something new or out of the ordinary that requires "coach" approval. There are times when you need to just take a break to clear your head of all the options and mental chatter and gain a better perspective regarding your next steps. It can be important to rest up and gain fresh energy for the final run to victory. Use your time outs wisely so you can maximize your effectiveness in the sales process.

Knowing When to Turn Up the Heat

The final area of game clock management is to know when the customer will have a higher probability to take action. There are key factors that are signs as to the willingness to take action and make a buying decision. Be on alert for the telling signs.

There are four signs that give you insight into the level of urgency you will employ in your clock management. These signs all involve the customer's perception of their current state. The first is when the customer is currently feeling good about their situation, yet are open to ideas that suggest that they could still improve. In this situation you will want to get to work on showing how much improvement will occur and that the return is higher than their current investment. There is a high probability that the customer will buy when the evidence of improvement is clear. Work your plan at a quick pace while the opportunity window is open.

The second situation is when the current results are greater than the customer expected or planned. There is little urgency on the part of the customer to change anything at this time. They are exceeding their expectations and are quite satisfied with their present situation. There is no reason to press this buyer for action; the risk is high that they will reject any offer you make. Therefore, this is more of a long-term situation. You will need to develop doubt or dissatisfaction in this customer's situation. Thus, preparing the groundwork for the new proposals that can customer's change budgets to prevent performance from waning.

The third situation is when a customer is very happy with their present or current perceived performance – even if you can see all kinds of problems and pitfalls in their current results. The key here is the customer has no clue as to the possibilities or the Peter Principle is alive and well, whereby this customer has reached their level of incompetence! Be careful with your time in this situation. If you push this person, they will reject you and create a negative image about you within the account. I refer to these situations as an attempt to convert the heathens! It is a total waste of your time. Your time would be better used developing other relationships within this organization. The reason is clear. This particular buyer, who seems to be in denial about their current situation, will eventually get called on the "carpet." At this time, the buyer usually moves into the fourth arena.

The fourth situation is the buyer knows that they are currently well below their desired performance. They have moved into crisis mode and are urgently looking for a solution to their problems or issues. This is the point that you want to raise the pace of working on an account. Why? Because this buyer has identified and admitted to pain! This buyer is actively looking for a cure to their source of pain. This buyer will make a fast decision and can push the pace to higher levels. Oh, three bids or RFP's will take too long for this customer – show them your solution and move to the close. Price is not the issue here; it's pain relief! Take immediate action steps with this account. If you hesitate someone else will get the deal.

One point of clarity about the above situations needs to be addressed. There is an assumption that the customers in these cases are all covered under the ideal customer profile. The business fit between your company and the customer are in total alignment. If the alignment is not there or the customer is outside your ideal customer profile, then your time is best spent elsewhere and it does matter which situation is in play.

Always remember that you control how you allocate and distribute the use of your time. Manage your game clock wisely for maximum productivity. The only thing that you can trade for sales success is your time.

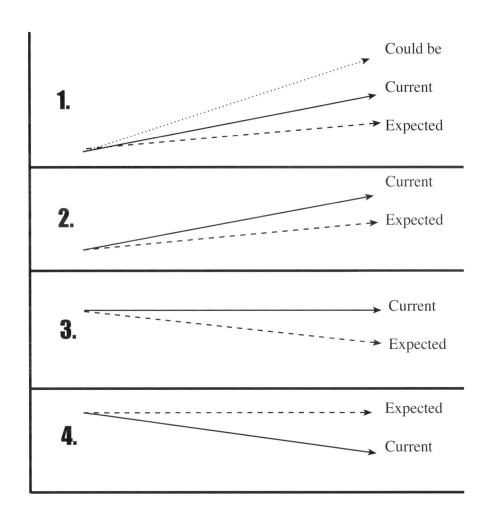

Coach Voss's Chalk Talk

Chapter Eight:
Managing the Game Clock

» *Winner's manage the clock all the time.*

» *Winner's create a sense of urgency to interact with customers.*

» *Loser's procastinate - waiting for the perfect moment.*

» *By managing the clock you create a postive reputation of consistency and results.*

» *Aligning a sales process with the customer's buying cycle improves success in selling.*

» *Calling time-outs can be an effective strategy for winning.*

» *Winner's compare actual and expected results and then decide whether to increase the contact with a customer.*

» *Think long-term for developing and accumulating talent.*

Chapter Nine

Half Time Adjustments

Winning football teams have a tendency to make excellent half-time adjustments that change the momentum of a game. The coaches and players make minor changes to their game play relative to things that have occurred on the field of play during the first half. In fact, the best teams make minor adjustments during the entire game to change the results being attained by their opponents. The changes can be minor or can be major alignment changes based upon the match-ups on the field of play.

The relationship to sales people and the use of half time adjustments is clear. As you begin to execute your plans, you will learn new information or challenges that the customer feels are more important than the information you had first uncovered doing research on the customer. This new information can create a need to rethink your objectives, tactics and strategies. It could make the opportunity larger or smaller. No matter what the ultimate situation is, you remain in control and make midcourse corrections to your plan.

The key here is not to be handcuffed or limited in scope due to a plan that you or your team developed. No plan should override common sense and the ability to think on your feet. Adaptability and flexibility are keys to a sales person's success. In fact, one of the top two reasons for failure is rigidity to any change. Plans are devices to be used as guides and tools for higher productivity, not as absolutes. Resist being taken prisoner by your own plans and planning process.

Let us look at this principle of adaptability. Winners are focused upon the big picture of how what they sell to their customers actually helps improve the customer's situation. If you only see the dollars from the sale or your commission check then you are missing a key mental image. The mental image that we are referencing is the higher purpose that puts you in the elite category. The elite class of sales people understands that they are selling to make a difference in their customer's lives. They live to serve their customers and create added value for both their customers and the company they are promoting. Using this as their mental model, the sale person moves down the sales process, noting their progress and learning more about their customer and the customer's business. When these true sales professionals are asked about their customers, they can tell you about their processes, the customer base, who their key accounts are and what impact they have on the customer, they can talk about the financial condition of the account, the goals and objectives of the key managers in the account, as well as what the issues are that keep the decision makers awake at night! As all this information is gathered, it is only natural to adjust your strategies and tactics based upon the customer issues rather than your need to sell something.

Make the necessary adjustments to maintain a long-term account relationship. Too often, sales people make short-term decisions to make a sale and lose the opportunity to gain the long-term business relationship. This type of decision will limit your overall success and place you in the middle of the commodity zone trap.

Another point to make concerning your half time adjustments is the concept of remaining customer focused. The focus is on the customer; yet, never lose site of the reason you are a sales person. Your job is to make sales and grow your company's top and bottom lines. The toughest assignment is to balance the competing needs of your company for immediate or short-term results and the needs of your customer. The customer needs are to have performance and productivity improvements provided by their business partners. Customers are not our enemies nor are they adversaries. The enemy is your competition who truly wants to beat you when competing for a customer's share of wallet. Treat your customers with dignity and respect. You will receive it back plus interest, not to mention referrals and references.

Another area for half time review is the overall strategy that you are using to develop an account relationship. Be prepared to adjust your strategy as things happen during the game. Examples of a need to change your strategy could be a major shake up in the management team, a merger, or the dreaded reorganization within the customer's world. These events will cause an immediate review of the strategy being used for that account. Any type of major change within the account demands a review of your strategy.

Tactics may be adjusted based upon a half time adjustment. If a sales team has been calling on a purchasing agent who has limited access to others within the company, then an adjustment in tactics must be considered. An example of tactical adjustments would be the use of a higher level officer making joint calls with the sales person to meet with higher level personnel at the account. Sometimes the use of marketing communications to develop interest from others within an account will open doors for new prospects and different combinations of products or services to be offered as business solutions to the customer.

The key to your success in sales is to be open to change and to make adjustments in your selling strategy or tactics. When a sales person is only one dimensional in the delivery of their products or services, he or she is limiting his or her possibilities. Our job is to create opportunities and improve the possibilities for success. Being adaptable and flexible in our approach to selling is our method and our choice for reaching the next level of success.

Coach Voss's Chalk Talk

Chapter Nine: Half Time Adjustments

» *Winners make excellent half time adjustments.*

» *Learning new information about your customer is the key for successful half time adjustment.*

» *No game plan is perfect - adjustments are necessary as more information is uncovered.*

» *Adaptability and Flexibility are key traits of successful sales people.*

» *Elite sales people think about the customer and their companies goals.*

» *Balance upon focus between short and long term objectives.*

» *Our main job is to create opportunities and improve the possibilities for winning.*

Chapter Ten

Working the Game Officials

There is a tendency for the best coaches and team captains to work the game officials during a game to enhance the probability of favorable calls during and at the end of the game.

In the world of selling, there is a clear need to work the game officials. However, in the world of selling, the game officials are not marked so you can clearly identify the officials from everyone else. The officials are the different buyer types, decision makers, buying influencers, blockers, and evaluators, as well as the classic gatekeepers. All these "officials" can have a direct or indirect impact on your success in selling to your accounts.

The Power of Networking

There are three primary areas to discuss concerning the best practices for working the game officials. The first area is networking. This is a simple way to meet and build relationships, yet it requires thought and more planning.

The industry that you are currently selling in will impact the methods that you use for effective networking. First, we have the basics of relating networking to building business relationships. You must target your networking opportunities so that they will enable you to meet the key players in your customer and prospect accounts. A little research goes a long way for your success. If you were a football coach, you would not be talking to the back judge if the lineman is the one causing all your problems with bad to questionable calls.

So, back to sales, what industry are you selling in for your current success? If you are in professional services in a local market, the selection is easy. Join the Chamber of Commerce in your town and attend the meetings. Make it your goal to meet as many people as possible within a stated period of time. The key is NO SELLING at the meetings. It is relationship-building time – no selling allowed. If you do fall in the trap of presenting yourself in a "telling all" mode, you are hurting your credibility in the process. The key is to learn about the customer or prospect, have conversational time with them, and ask questions to gain clarity about them. Remember, networking is about them, not you. The fastest way for someone to be interested in you is for you to be interested in him or her. Too often we focus our attention on ourselves and lose the opportunity to gain a true relationship.

Okay, let's move up the chain of networking. If you sell to a specific industry using a regional focus, then check into trade associations for the industry and learn if there is a regional chapter. Join the chapter or at a minimum attend their meetings, get on their mailing lists, or write an article for their newsletter. Sometimes a sales person is asked to speak to an industry group. If you are asked, then say yes.

Remember to deliver a neutral presentation; it is not a product or service demonstration that they want. They want insight to the industry and ways to improve their situation, so give them what they want. How do you get this neutral information? Use actual case studies (without any actual names) and tell the story. A story is the most powerful communication tool that we have to offer. If you have any experience under your belt, you will have many stories to offer. Life is filled with stories that deliver meaning and purpose for others.

If you sell on more of a national basis, then you will want to join the national trade associations that your customers and prospects would join. This will allow you to learn more about them and their industry. If you are having trouble finding this information there are three ways to learn about possible groups. First, ask your current customers about the organizations they participate in and the advantages they seek through their membership. Second, contact or search the web for the National Association of Wholesale Distributors. This is an organization that represents all the different trade associations and offers important lobbying and research about the wholesale (business to business) industry. And the third area is the web. Use sites like Google.com or Yahoo.com for general information searches. Another site that will help you identify trade associations is Northernlight.com, which is the best source for articles from hundreds of trade associations. This is an excellent source for learning about the trends in the industry that you are currently selling, as well as any potential new industry you have picked to sell.

Other more general areas for networking can be civic organizations like the Rotary, Lions, and Kiwanis clubs. As a member of your local group, you can attend meetings in other cities or states and meet the key individuals within that local area. If you sell primarily to the top or "C" class within your accounts then you also need to look at civic, charity, and non-profit organizations. The leaders of the communities have a sense of pride in their communities and will volunteer their services to certain organizations that they personally believe are important. Groups that get key managers to work with them include the United Way, the Boy or Girl Scout organizations, the Red Cross, the Little or Community Theatre, Botanical Gardens or Zoos, and Business Development Committees for the local or regional economic zones. The key is to take some time and explore the networking opportunities within your selling environment. Look at membership rosters and find out where your contacts are most likely to be outside of their corporate environment. Finally, one word of caution is necessary at this point. It is more effective if you choose organizations that you have a personal interest or passion to participate in and promote. It is important to join and participate in the group's purpose. The goal is to find active connections rather than see how many organizations you can list on your bio. Take an active position and watch how others will respond to your authenticity.

Knowing Who to Call

The second area of importance in working the game officials, is knowledge of who the game officials are in your accounts. It is still amazing to watch a sales person continue to call on the wrong people in an organization and actually expect them to buy! One of your major job responsibilities is to call on the right people in your account organizations. So how do you find out who the right people are?

There are four areas to consider in evaluating whom to focus on during your sales process. The first area is to look at those in certain positions or who have certain titles. While this is usually an easy task, it does not provide the most accurate information regarding the actual decision maker for your sales process. Titles are just titles, the true responsibility for making a buying decision can be located in multiple areas within a company. Now if you are calling at the top, as a strategy, it is usually better to be coming from the top levels. To call at the top, it would be important to learn the names of the people with a certain titles. The President, CEO, CFO, CIO, and COO can be identified using the web or a direct call to the company. As you move down into the organization, you will find more titles – Executive VP, Senior VP, Vice President, Division Managers, Materials Managers, General Managers, Director level, Manager of various departments or functions, and various project or team leaders that could be involved in the decision process of your sale, not to mention anyone in the purchasing department. The titles are not guarantees of decision-making power or responsibility. Many times a sales person will call on the President of a company and believe they have the real decision maker in the bag only to learn too late that the real decision maker was the Division VP! Therefore, titles should be used only as a guide for identifying the decision maker for your efforts.

The next area to use in your evaluation of learning who the decision maker will be, is to think about who makes this type of decision in similar companies that you have successfully sold. While there is no guarantee that other companies will be structurally set up the same way, it also can be used as a guide for learning who could be the real decision maker. In fact, one way a sales person can lose is to attempt to sell to the same person all the time. This limited point of view will hurt you in at least three ways. The first is you get into a comfort zone of only calling on the same person, and therefore you limit the network of contacts within the customer or prospects business. You actually become dependent on this one person for your sales success within this account and your vulnerability to losing it becomes higher than you realize.

The second is that it limits the number of insights and options that you can use in developing account strategies and possible solution offerings. If all your information is coming from a single source (even if it is the President of the company), their filters and biases can be an issue in learning about the true or objective situations that you are charged to improve. There are sales processes that have failed during implementation due to a lack of either key information or key personnel involvement in the creation of solutions. Beware of the consequences of limited sources for vital and key information. The third area for evaluating whom you should be calling upon in a selling situation is to look carefully at the specific sales objective, then think about whom this decision impacts the most? This simple process will assist you in aligning your sales strategy with the person most influential towards making the decision. The key in this evaluation is to give thought to the critical relationships between the buying decision criteria and the performance expected from the execution of the decision. It is important to do this exercise due to the fact that the specific solution you are engaging to sell may use many different combinations of influencers. To think whomever you sold to previously in an account will be the same people evaluating, testing and making a decision concerning your newest sales proposal is what we call an errant assumption. Errant assumptions are the root cause of all poor decisions according to Peter Drucker in his book *The Effective Executive*. Making an assumption as to whom the players are in the decision making process is okay as long as you validate your assumptions! We have seen situations where a sales person is making multiple sales offerings within an account to multiple decision makers for the same products and services; yet, the buying responsibilities rest with unrelated job titles.

The final and fourth area of identifying the right people to approach for the decision making process is your internal coach's network. The concept of having an internal coach is an important aspect in selling to business organizations. An internal account coach provides you with a couple of clear advantages. First, a coach usually wants you to win. They want to help you make the sale, and therefore will provide you with valuable insight into their company. The second advantage is that the coach can provide you with insider information. Now, I'm not talking about illegal stock traders' information! What is important is the insider's knowledge of how things are done, what are the political issues you will encounter, and who are the real players, influencers and blockers within the account? By helping you to understand who is playing which role in the organization or in your buying decision, you will improve your tactical strategies in the engagement of developing allies in your sales process.

Having just one internal coach is very similar to just calling on the same person at an account. Your goal is to develop a network of internal coaches within your accounts. Now if you are only selling to very small accounts then the decision maker, evaluator and coach may be the same person! However, in most accounts you will want to develop multiple coaches and the larger the account the more the coach becomes a necessity.

There are several advantages to having multiple coaches. First, there is the factor of familiarity with different work groups, departments, or divisions. I have not found one person that truly understands everything that goes on within an organization. However, within their immediate work area they have an insider's insight. The second is you can detect trends when you begin to hear the same information coming from multiple sources. If only one person is saying something, there is a higher probability that it is a personal bias or opinion that is not backed by facts. If you follow this lead too fast, you could get burned. How? If the internal coach is not highly regarded in the organization or has lost their prestige within the organization, you run the risk of negative branding due to association. Another advantage is that you can choose whose advice you will follow based upon their total knowledge of the situation. It's similar to the buying committee following the lead of the dominant buyer or influencer. You can choose whose action suggestion is the best for your objective. The final advantage is the old "safety in numbers" approach to doing business. The more coaches you have, the less vulnerable you become to reorganizations, downsizing situations, or retirements. It is important to have multiple coaches even in smaller organizations. Larger organizations require that you develop both influencer networks and coach networks to win the multiple opportunities that will be presented to you.

The Role of Positive Communication

The third key factor in working the game officials is the power of positive communication. There are two primary areas that we need to focus on concerning positive communications. The first area deals specifically with the fact that positive information will create an environment that leads to more collaboration with customers than a stream of negative information.

We know that some people feel that positive thinking alone will get the job done. Or they believe that by being enthusiastic they will overcome every obstacle in their path to success. Well, while there is merit to these concepts, the truth lies somewhere in between. Positive knowing is a better place to come from than just positive thinking due to the certainty of having dealt with issues or problems in the past. Possessing a level of experience will bring a degree of reality into both thoughts and actions. The only element of enthusiastic attitude that truly helps a sales person is the degree of optimism that they possess. This element determines how your customer will interpret your communications. A "can do or will do" attitude becomes the norm in the relationship. A sales person's word selection meshes with his or her attitude about his or her customers and how well the sales person provides real service levels to the customer. An optimist's attitude will be open to looking for ways to make a solution work, while a pessimist will be looking for the reasons it will not work or fail. How do you talk to your customers? Do you take responsibility for framing the possibilities for success or do you sound more like a CYA memo? You will ultimately set the framework for your customer to do business with you. Therefore, do you set it up for success or failure? Speak using positive language that sets you up for results you want to have.

The Role of Positive Language is important to your overall and long-term success. Therefore it is important that we clarify one major point. We are not asking you to take a Pollyanna approach in your communications. Not all things can be done well and some things need not be done at all! What is important is your responsibility to take ownership in your language and communication skills. Too many people lack the proper understanding of effectiveness in their communication with others. Take the time to learn how to be more effective. Learn about the different styles and preferences used by people so you can match their preferred communication style. Learn the importance of phrasing and word selection for more effectiveness in understanding. Learn to avoid lazy or general language techniques that inhibit effectiveness in personal interaction. Remember that you are responsible for the effectiveness of your messages – so make everything count!

Another important aspect of communication for working the game officials is the use of a systematic or programmed information campaign. In business-to-business selling, this concept has moved to the front row of execution. Why? Because our customers have no time to listen to uninformed sales people who are willing to waste the customer's time with blah-blah-blah product pitches! Due to the commodity effect, our products and services will sound just alike to the harried customer. Therefore, we must use a strategy and implement our strategy with tactics that will differentiate our products and services from the thunderhead of "me-to" products and services.

One method is to use a systematic campaign to educate our customers on the uniqueness of our product and services. How do we do this? Using a combination of face to face visits, direct mail and email, we deliver good news about how we are helping so many other companies and people to improve their working situation. We talk about business issues and how we have solved or improved these issues for others "just like you." We can even place very specific information in the campaign to show that we understand what is troubling them. The most valuable statement a customer can say to you is "It's a pleasure doing business with someone that really understands my business!" This phrase is the golden message. The customer believes in you and you have gained their trust.

The use of a systematic campaign requires that you plan the approaches and the messages. In summary, the process works when you take the time to plan your strategy. You must identify what problems your products and services solve for your customers. Then you move to the issues that your customers are experiencing or what trends will cause implementation issues for your customers. Then you marry what you solve to the issues the customers are dealing with or you anticipate they will be dealing with in the near future. Actually, a good trend recognition process will be very valuable to you since you can be the first person to identify ways to fix situations. By identifying an "up and coming" trend, you can position yourself with multiple messages as the trend "fix-it" person. So when the trend impacts the results of the customer, you will be the top-of-mind solution. This is a very favorable position to establish in the customer's mind. You automatically become more valuable to the customer and in some cases they don't know why – they just know you can help them in their time of need.

So, you have identified the problems you fix, the issues for your customers, and have given thought to both whom and how you will communicate with your customers and targeted prospects. Now comes the hard part, the execution of this process sounds like it will take a lot of manual work. Well the answer is yes – if you do it manually. Here is the time to take advantage of technology! Technology was invented to perform the standardized tasks or repetitive work that some of us really do not care to do on a regular basis. There is software available that will automate the campaign process for you so that an administrative person or sales coordinator can process the multiple letters and emails for the sales person.

Now it does take time to identify your targeted accounts, target contacts within these accounts, and prepare a targeted message for delivering a clear, positive position statement for delivery. If the message is well written, the contact can relate to and take action when they need a solution. Therefore, it is important to do this part as part of your overall planning process. Make the tough decisions, get the software that can handle automated campaigns, get the customer database established, and either write or have written the letters or emails by a marketing communications expert.

The key is to make consistency of message, position, and contact with your customers your action goal. This tactical strategy will place you in a category called "top-of-mind." This establishes you as the person to call about " X." X being whatever or however you have positioned yourself. The important thing to remember is, that due to the consistent contact, the customer will call you at the exact moment that they need to fix or improve the issue when it moves to the front burner on their priority stove. Be prepared to respond with a sense of urgency when they call since they are ready to move forward and will not be taking three bids!

Campaigns are very effective when you are in major accounts, have specific targeted accounts, have a large geographical territory or market, and you are engaged in business-to-business selling. Retail and business-to-consumer selling can utilize this technique, yet it becomes a more direct mail based practice. In this approach, the ability to target a market niche and knowledge of how to find or process data-base listings for the direct mail pieces becomes more impor-tant. The major differences between a general direct mail piece and the targeted market campaign is the ability to sig-nificantly improve the response rates in the targeted campaign over the general direct mail piece.

Your success depends upon your ability to get in front of the right people at the right time with the right offering. Working the game officials is the way that you improve your probability of success in being at the right place at the right time with the right package.

In summary, establish a plan for networking and execute your plan. The level and degree of active participation will depend upon what you sell and to whom you sell. Yet, have a plan for networking. As a salesperson, your success does depend upon whom you know as well as what you know! Develop a process for identifying the people that are the decision makers. A network of internal coaches will assist you in this process and will prove to be invaluable to you in the long run. And finally, develop a positive message that is consistently delivered to the right players. This practice will influence the buyers toward you, due to higher levels of trust, a perception of expertise, and confidence that you can deliver the results that they are looking for at this time.

Coach Voss's Chalk Talk

Chapter Ten:
Working the Game Officials

» *Officials carry both a direct and indirect impact upon your success - manage them wisely.*

» *Networking allows you to be known, to know others and evaluate talent.*

» *Credibility is earned through hard work.*

» *Knowing which official to call upon improves your winning percentages.*

» *Working only one official can limit effectiveness.*

» *Validating your assumptions improves your decision making process.*

» *Share information and knowledge with key officials (without selling) to gain credibility.*

» *Positive communication elevates the probability of favorable decisions.*

» *Your goal is to become "top of mind" as a good person to work with during a critical game.*

Chapter Eleven

Using Your Two Minute Drill

When college football teams enter the last phase of each game, a clear execution strategy shows up as the game clock winds down to zero. Depending upon the score and which team has the ball, you begin to see very different tactics. The team with the lead will become very conservative in their offensive tactics. In fact, their strategy will focus on keeping the clock running as fast and long as possible to end the game with the lead. If the team with the ball is behind, you begin to see very aggressive offensive strategy. The passing offense comes to life and the four and five receiver packages are utilized in an attempt to score and score fast.

Defenses are also affected during this last couple of minutes. If the team on defense is behind, a gambling, high-risk blitz package can be given the green light, particularly when the score is tight. This package has been referred as looking like a jail break with defensive players coming from all directions in an attempt to cause a major mistake by the offensive team. Since the term "high-risk" is used, it is clear that there is no guarantee of success.

Sales people need to be aware and prepared for their own two minute drill. Which tactics a sales person will use depends upon whether he or she is ahead in the sales process or behind in the sales process. With either position, the sales person must be prepared to take action, in order to take control of his or her own success.

We will explore the end game of selling looking at two primary positions.

"You're Leading the Game" Tactics

The first primary position is the best position. You are ahead in the sales process and are considered the front runner. There are four possible action strategies for the sales person that is ahead in the sales process.

The first action strategy is to do nothing. Here the sales person is counting on the system to take care of him or her. This is a high risk approach that assumes your competition will take no action to overtake you. This is one of those errant assumptions we reviewed earlier. Your competition will be working harder than ever to find any opening to delay the decision, or reopen the sales process with new specifications, new information, or new situations that will change the playing field dynamics. Losing sales people use the "do nothing" strategy too often! There are factors in play by losing sales people creating this passive approach. One is that they have low self-esteem and feel they are unworthy of this success. They actually feel that the only reason they are in front is luck! And since they believe in bad luck they are now waiting for the proverbial "other shoe to fall." The second reason is one of arrogance.

This deadly attitude can cause a sale to fall apart at the last moment. When a sales person shows arrogance to either the competition or their customer, the ball is set in motion for an upset! When the customer senses this attitude, their trust levels drop and uncertainty enters the game. The most common tactic used by the customer when arrogance is recognized is the sudden stall in the sales process. The clearest signal is missed deadlines at critical closing milestones. Other people begin to enter the playing field, usually for the first time, and the sales person takes no action to meet these people or learn about any new issues or concerns. Then, someone else wins the game! It's like the "Hail Mary pass" play that works on the last play of the game, and while it is called a miracle play, the fact is it happened because someone lost focus at a critical juncture of the game.

The second tactic for the sales person who is ahead in the sales process is to continue to use the same game plan until the end. This plan will work most of the time unless the sales person gets too aggressive. While aggressiveness or assertiveness will get you ahead in many games, this behavioral style will become too risky at the end of the game.

In college football games, we often see a team take the same aggressive approach in the last minutes of the game and lose due to errors and mistakes at critical times. A turnover deep in their own end of the field leading to a touchdown or field goal and then big "mo" (an emotional part of the game that changes momentum from one team to another.) takes over for the competitor and the results suddenly change.

The key for a sales person's success is to continue to focus on the goal of the customer winning. This focus on the customer rather than on you will allow for continuity of actions. These actions should always be focused on the customer's improvement and growth. Focus and clarity of actions will keep you error free during the end game.

One of the downside issues, about which the sales person needs to be aware, concerns the primary behavioral style of the decision maker or primary buyer. Some of these people will have a very non-confrontational style. When you encounter this behavioral style, the key to your success is to seldom push this style. Why? Because they will use passive-aggressive actions to counter your aggressiveness. This means they will actually delay the closing of a deal or contract. At the same time, they will become unavailable for meetings with you. It is during this time that your competition can score points with the customer and thereby knock you out of the lead. This is a common error made by assertive sales people. The rule is to sell to people the way they want to be sold.

The third tactic a sales person can use is to burn the clock as fast as you can. This means that you remain in contact with your customer and several of the influencers and coaches during the end stage of the sales process. Be available to answer questions. Treat each question like it could be a deal- breaker, because it could be a deal-breaker if you ignore it. The key here is to listen to every question, listen to what is said, and what is not said that should have been said based upon your experience. Ask clarifying questions to gain a true understanding for the basis of each question.

Consistently reaffirm the advantages of the customer doing business with you and your company. Another behavioral style issue can be addressed at this stage. Depending upon the dominant behavioral style of the decision maker or key influencer, you will emphasize different factors as you reassure them about the upcoming decision. The hard charging, pure business-type will like hearing about the results they will get. The outgoing, talkative, and enthusiastic type will like to hear how the decision will make them look and feel good, as well as being appreciated for their decision. The systematic doer with the friendly attitude will like to hear how the decision will allow them to get along with others in his or her organization. The fact finding, detailed, and critical listener type of person will like to hear how a favorable decision will make things right and is the best choice given the available information. The sales person who is aware of the conditions and factors involved in the sales and buying process will adjust their tactics to insure success.

By staying engaged with the customer and showing a helpful action orientation, the sales person will stay the course and improve the percentages for success. Losers increase their chances for failure by losing focus and disengaging with the customer at a critical stage.

Your mindset during the end stages is very important. Do you play to win? Or do you play not to lose? This is a very critical differentiating factor for the sales person. A college football team in my home town had a head coach who was a class act person, and everyone who knew him felt that he was a good person and truly wanted his team to experience winning. Yet, his teams had a losing record every year. Why? Because his mental mindset was based upon "playing not to lose." This factor led to his dismissal since moral victories cannot offset continuously losing to teams with less talent. His teams set a record for losing games in the fourth quarter based upon going too conservative on both offense and defense. The preventive defense in his case actually prevented his team from winning rather than maintaining a lead! His attitude of playing not to lose was mirrored in the attitudes and actions of his teams. They would start fast, doing the unexpected and get a lead in the first half. This would give the team and fans hope until the fourth quarter when a new team would show up and lose the game – often in dramatic and creative ways!

So what does this mean to a sales person entering the last stage of the sales process? It means that your mental condition will impact your actions and behaviors leading to either victory or defeat. Control your thoughts, and your actions will follow. Keep a positive outlook for success and take actions to engage the customer. This engagement action will show the customer that you are an action-oriented person capable of leading both of you to victory. Win-win is your dominant approach to doing business and the customer will make certain that you are the winner.

The fourth tactic for the sales person in the lead is to get the officials to call the game early. This is a similar strategy that football teams take to kill the clock by having the quarterback take a knee and letting the clock expire. We want the game officials to let the clock expire.

This happens most often when the sales person has done an excellent job of getting to the final stage. The sales person has not rushed or pushed for a sale, yet, has uncovered all the issues and concerns of the customer, positioned solutions and created a sense of urgency using questions so the customer self-discovers the importance of a timely decision. In other words, the customer is ready and willing to close the deal and make a decision. This shuts out the competition and moves the sale or the account business relationship to the next level of implementation. This strategy started at the first moment of thought about the customer by the winning sales person. It involves a total sales process that engages the customer from the opening and maintains a positive stress level for taking the corrective action for improvement. Without a focused sales process that separates the sales person from the thundering herd of competitors, the results would become more haphazard. The top football programs and the top sales people maintain an attitude of expecting to win. While expecting to win is a driver, they then set out to insure their success by preparing for the long haul. They do not "wing it" on the practice field or during game conditions. They are focused and execute their plan even in the face of adversity.

"You're Behind in the Game" Tactics

If you are behind in the game, your approach is different. Here, your strategy is to lengthen the game or extend the game clock until you can score. While at first glance this appears to be a defensive strategy, it is based upon a new offensive plan with an optimized package of risk and excellent execution.

There are four tactics to be employed in the "getting back in the game" approach to sales success. The first is give up and play another game tactic. This is not rocket science and is the most often used approach by both top people and losers with one major difference. The new strategy or tactic is perfectly okay, and then the game is totally out of reach for some reason. The winning football teams that find themselves out of a game in the last few minutes usually got in that position due to a series of costly errors – usually in the form of turnovers that led to easy or quick scores by the opponent, or by a couple of big plays for touchdowns in the form of punt returns or deep pass plays for touchdowns. Now, the difference in approach between the top teams and losing teams is that the top teams play for both pride and re-establishing their dominant behavioral style in the closing minutes in preparation for the next game. The losers tend to lose focus and concentration, whereby the opponent usually gets a couple of "cheap" scores leading to a blowout game.

Sales people need to maintain an attitude of the winners and prepare for the next game. In some cases they actually got to the game late, so their strategy is to set the stage for the next game with the customer. Show your winning attitude and begin the process for the next sale. Losers just leave and do no work to prepare themselves or the customer for the next game. They just give up! Sales people need to remember what Winston Churchill said during World War II, "Never, Never Give Up!" By applying the "never give up" attitude to your sales process, you can lead yourself to more wins. In the game of selling, second place is not a good thing!

The strategy used by sales people to get back in the game is to use your natural or established strengths with an occasional use of a surprise tactic. In college football, a team may be excellent at running the football and possess a strong offensive line with several talented running backs. Their strength is running the ball. During the course of the game, they have gone to a passing attack due to several factors like turnovers or they have given the opponent several quick scores, or the opponent's defense was placing "nine men in the box" to shut down the running game. As the fourth quarter starts, the coach decides that the team needs to use their strength and run the ball. So the process begins of running the ball; yet, remember the defense, they have prepared for the run with a "nine man in the box" defense. Therefore, it is necessary to add a "surprise" to the attack. The surprise usually comes in the form of a play action pass whereby the offense fakes a running play and a pass is thrown over the "nine man" at the line of scrimmage. Most of the time a receiver is open and the play results in big yardage and scores. This surprise tactic is used to force the opponent out of their tactical strategy by taking advantage of their weakness.

In the world of selling a sales person must be aware of their personal strengths, their company's strengths, and their product or service offerings' strengths. By knowing their strengths, they can leverage these strengths to gain a competitive advantage and take the competition out of their strategy. However if you do not know your strengths, then this tactic is of little value to you. Find out what your strengths are and use these strengths as you enter the final phase of the sales process. Remind the customer of the advantages of working with you, your company, and your product or service. Counter the competitor's position with both business and personal reasons showing the ways the customer wins using you.

The surprise factor in this tactic is to offer something late in the game to test the waters and verify if the customer is actually open to new tactics or new information. Now most sales people assume that the surprise is another cut in price. Only a limited one-time "special" offer should be used as a price incentive. There are other and more creative ways to surprise the customer at the end. Some sales people use special product training for the customer, offers to train the customer's customer, private label packaging using the customers name and logo, additional joint advertising incentives or programs, and other "unique to the customer" packages that have not been offered in the past. The key is to get creative and think of ways to offset the competitor's position. Your creativity is your big play tool, so use it often.

The third tactic for getting back in the game is concentrated effort. Here the tactic is to get everyone involved and get the momentum back in the sales process. This tactic works for football teams when the team leaders get the team refocused on winning, staying focused, and expecting to find a way to win the game. A new level of effort springs from all parts of the team, and they find a way to change the flow of momentum and take the game back to their side of the field. This tactic is the source of several old clichés like "When the going gets tough, the tough get going!" The key is to believe that you can make a difference no matter the circumstances or obstacles that are placed in your pathway. Just do it!

A sales person using the concentrated effort tactic means that they use a sense of urgency combined with a new focus on getting results. A bias for action becomes the important thing for this sales person. They get involved in getting additional information about the customer that could change the solution offered. They call on other people in the customer's organization to gain more allies for the solution. They get other people from their company involved in the customer calls, they have technical people call on the customer's technical people, they have the sales manager meet with higher level people in the customer's organization, and sometimes get " C – level" officers to call on the customer's top people to show the combined commitment to making the relationship a high priority for both companies.

Refocusing your efforts is an excellent tactic for showing the customer that they are very important to you. It shows that you will not disappear when things become difficult in a customer relationship. It shows the true character the sales person possesses and enhances the trust development needed for true business relationships to flourish.

The last of the four tactics is the most radical and does require a level of risk taking on the part of the sales person. This tactic is the New Strategy approach. This is only used when the overall feeling and analysis shows that you are seriously behind in the game, yet you are not ready to give up and quit the game. When it's established that there is a high probability you are losing, you have little to risk if you change tactics and strategy near the end of the sales process and the buyer's buying cycle.

Let's assume that your tactical strategy has been to only call on the purchasing group and they have told you not to go around them. If you feel that they are going to award a competitor the business, and you know that your offering or solution is a better fit for the customer, then it is decision time. You could enter the customer's account at a new level and use different tactics in discussing a higher level solution that matches a real business objective of the higher level people in the customer's organization. It is possible that your actions will cause issues with the purchasing group that did not want you meeting with others; however, these same people were blocking you out of the game in the first place! It will not hurt you more than you are already hurt, so change the game. "Changing the game" should be the title of this tactic. Change is good when it is self-directed with a goal or objective in mind. Then you implement the change you have planned.

The game of selling has been changing for a couple of decades, yet, most sales people have been so engaged in the tactical or traditional side of the game that new and more effective tactics still go unused today. Be prepared to change the game based on your strengths and how you actually need to play the game to reach your goals and objectives. Beware of the opponents wanting you to play their game rules. Purchasing agents often create their own personal game rules and threaten you to play their game. Why? It makes them feel important and the power feels good. If you think about what a buyer actually does for their company it becomes clear. They are asked or told to buy certain things (the real authority is coming from somewhere else in the organization), so they are just following orders. These orders include buying at the lowest price. Therefore, value added selling is not important to them. So the rules of their game are established with the dual objectives of feeling important (when others in their own organization do not always have the same objective) and meeting the results of their job in getting the lowest price. So unless you are the low price king, you are playing the wrong game! Change the strategy and sell business alignment at higher levels in the organization.

If you are already selling to the higher levels in your customer accounts, and you use "change the game", tactical strategy takes on a new dimension. If you are losing in the fourth quarter, have you determined the real issue that is keeping you from the winning side of the field? You cannot solve the issue until you have identified the issue. This is using the Law of Cause and Effect. Find the true cause, change your tactics, and you will get a new effect.

We have found too many sales people that want different results or effects; yet, they refuse to change the causes. This is the true definition of insanity – expecting different results using the same old methods and tactics. Take new actions or develop new strategies for winning more business. The information is available for you to change. You must decide to take the necessary actions to get new results.

A key factor in this "change the game" tactical strategy is that the sales person needs more alternatives or options relative to the situations they encounter. This is like a software program that contains a drop down list box for filling in a database item. The fewer options you have, the easier the choice, yet, is it a good choice? It is important to increase your number of options so you can choose the most appropriate choice for the situation you are currently dealing with in the marketplace. Attempting to deal with all situations using a limited number of options or alternatives is the fastest way to join the losing team. Learn and think about different ways to achieve your results and you will be a member of a top team every year.

In summary, as a sales person, you want to be prepared going into the last phases of the sales process. Practice different tactics depending upon whether you are behind or ahead in the process. Apply the tactic that matches the real situation and improve your results. Again, "winging-it" is for losers, practice your new approaches in a safe environment, and then execute on the real game field – the customer's office.

Coach Voss's Chalk Talk

Chapter Eleven: Using the 2 Minute Drill

» *Tactics change based upon your evaluation of the "score."*

» *When leading, maintain contact in a conservative manner.*

» *Always Play to Win.*

» *Playing not to lose guarantees a creative way to lose.*

» *Sell to customers the way "they" want to be sold - insures victory.*

» *Get the game called early by working your plan so well - the customer signs the purchase order.*

» *When losing - play with pride and set yourself up for the next game / customer.*

» *A bias for action keeps you in the game.*

» *Never, NEVER Give up!*

» *Changing the game is a tactic to overcome the established odds - and win.*

Chapter Twelve

The Extra Point

An interesting analogy to life is the extra point after a touchdown is scored. First, most people think that the extra point kick is an automatic point. However, in reality we find that this is not the case. It is true that a high percentage of success is found in the extra point attempt, yet, why is it?

Well, the extra point is considered a chip shot of only 18 yards and is positioned in the center of the goal posts. So, what goes wrong in an extra point attempt? First, there is the snap of the football to the holder – if it is off a couple of degrees in any direction, the timing of the kick is off. Is the holder for the extra point capable of catching the ball and placing it at the point of contact with the laces in the right direction, angle correct and the finger pressure on the top of the football just right? Then, there is the lineman who must hold off the competition to give the kicker time to kick. The coordination and timing of the extra point is all in the details.

So how does this compare to sales? It's all about customer satisfaction and service. Many organizations and sales people take this element for granted – just like the extra point. Yet, this is a critical part of the overall customer retention process. How well does the team work together to keep a customer satisfied with the product or service. It is all about the details of execution.

When a customer agrees to buy from you, this is the point that the customer begins to rely upon you and your company to deliver. The customer has agreed to your solution and now expects you to deliver - as agreed. At this point, the special teams (using our football analogy) enters the field of play. The accounting people, the shipping personnel, the support personnel, technical staff, supply chain personnel and all the other functional personnel involved in the transaction are now on the field.

If you or your organization are not on the same page regarding the execution of this all- important special team activity, then you are at risk of losing the hard earned "score" – the business you expect from the customer. The key is to coordinate this all important phase of the sale. The superstars of selling take the time to deliver relationships in these functional areas to insure proper execution for your customers. The low performers leave this phase of the business to chance or just expect it to be automatic.

Make it your goal to maintain personal contacts in the important functional areas so the details of execution are covered and you win all the close games. The worst feeling in the world is to lose due to faulty execution of a routine play. Remember to check your assumptions about what is routine and who is in a position to assist you at a critical junction in your business success.

A Special Extra Point Note for Sales Managers

Sales managers are like the coaching staff of college football teams. They are responsible for setting goals and expectations, developing game plans and strategies, coaching techniques and proper execution, performance reviews (game film), evaluating personnel and consistent recruitment of new players.

The evaluating existing talent and recruitment of new players/sales people is one of the critical factors for long term success in your sales organization. We suggest that you use the zero based thinking analysis to the existing sales team. This process starts by thinking about the qualities and characteristics and performance of the existing sales team members. Then, mentally note, "knowing what I know to be true today, would I hire this person today?" If the answer is yes, then classify as an A, B or C player and identify their individual strengths and weaknesses. If the answer is "no," then you need to discover the reasons why and decide to take action regarding these sales people. The actions include three options: 1. Dehire the person immediately and cut your loses; 2. Place the individual on probation and set up an immediate improvement plan; or 3. Reassign the person to another area that fits the person's strengths and allow the person to continue contributing to the organization.

The second area of critical importance is the consistent recruitment of high performance talent. The highest level college football programs consistently recruit players with the highest levels of talent. The potential recruits are tested at camps and combines before an offer is presented. The speed, strength, IQ, technique and skills are tested and retested for accuracy. Then the character test is applied, before an offer is extended.

Our experience has shown the same process is used by excellent sales managers. The process you should be using includes the following steps. (For a complete overview of the hiring process go to www.hiringsaleswinners.com) Check the resumes (knowing that some of the information on the resume many not be totally accurate.) and verify as much information as you can. Check the references asking good questions like "Would you hire this person again?" and listen to the response. Use telephone interviews to eliminate and reduce the number of candidates to the qualified few. Have an assessment process that gives you objective information regarding how the person will sell, what motivates them to sell, do they have to will to sell and what level of sales skills do they possess. By learning about what makes a sales person succeed, you are able to make better decisions regarding the quality of talent, short and long term potential and how to manage both your expectations and the sales person's expectations in the work environment. Finally, use behavioral interview questions to gain clarity and understanding regarding the level of talent possessed by the individual. Put them in situational role plays and listen for their experience, thought process and decision making abilities.

Remember, the quality of the talent you recruit will have a direct and long-lasting impact upon your job. Your credibility as a sales manager is in direct proportion to the talent you recruit and retain on your sales team. Use a structure or process that improves your probability of success. Do not take this area for granted – losers just line up and attempt the extra point with no thought, practice or plan. Be a winner, have a special teams mentality and put in the effort, practice and strategies. Again, the details and extra effort gives you the competitive edge.

Game Evaluation

The Economic Scouting Report

Overview

The Economic Scouting Report

The world of selling has changed. Some people and organizations have seen the light and are making the right moves to prepare for success in their fields of play. Others continue to use old and out-dated methods and tactics in an effort to overwhelm the opponent – who usually is the customer rather than the competition.

During the mid 90's, I was working with sales organizations and providing sales development for their sales teams. As I continued to teach the skill sets for effective selling, I was continually challenged by the sales people on three fronts: 1) What I was teaching them was working very well with some customers and was failing with other customers that looked just like their best customers. 2) Their own sales managers or higher level managers would challenge the new ways with policies, memos, or actions that made it difficult to stay the course. And 3) when they were successful, their business grew so fast that other departments would be overwhelmed and create new types of issues for the sales people to handle.

Due to this continuing array of issues and challenges, I began to scout the field of play looking for answers that could provide solutions, tactics, and strategies for effective results. What I found changed the way I provided information and development for sales teams and sales managers.

This problematic situation is actually created due to two separate forces of economic philosophy running parallel in our society and business environments. At first, these new truths were labeled as the New School and the Old School of business philosophies. In the world of sports we can compare them to the old three yards and a cloud of dust running game of football to the new wide open spread passing offenses that believe that the pass sets up the running plays. These football philosophies are as different as the New School and Old School of Business. Understanding these philosophies of business is not limited to the sales arena. My experience shows that by using this knowledge you can improve the opportunities for success in all business functions.

Let's look at the two schools of thought and identify the major elements including the mental mindsets found in each school of thought and how they impact the actions of people and organizations. The major elements that are covered include management issues, selling issues, communication priorities and structural factors for companies in each Model.

Old School

The Traditional Model of Business

The Old School of Business, which we now call the Traditional Model, is the backbone of the Industrial Age of Business. In order for the traditional model to operate at peak levels of efficiency, certain "laws" of business or characteristics were developed for this model to survive in its world. Let's take a look at each factor within this model. *See Graph One.*

Major Theme

The major theme within the Traditional Model of Business is "to persuade." From the top position on down, the people of the traditional organization are using persuasion to get things done. Very little listening is involved since the organizational chart rules the day and each level tells the next level what to do – no questions asked. Similar to the traditional family approach where the parent tells the child "to just do it because I told you." Efficiency is the name of the game since the manager is all knowing and does not want to waste any time explaining or taking the time to learn if others understand what is needed or how to do it. Persuasion was the tactic of choice and was used by management on the employees, and sales people used it on their customers.

Focus

The major focus is on the company's product or service offered. Using this strategy or tactic, insures that everything revolves around the product or service provided by the company. With the combination of the "to persuade" theme coupled with the focus being placed firmly upon their product, the company adopts an attitude of "We know what is good for the customer!" This combination saved organizations well during the economic times when demand for products and services outpaced actual supply. So companies were able to sell everything that they could produce, and efficiency was a key factor for success in their business world. Customer influence was largely a waste of time and effort and was not encouraged nor tolerated by managers.

Management Style

Command and control was the most popular management method of the traditional company. Since the economic environment was less complex for the traditional company, when they were the only game on the globe, command and control was easy for the best managers. Less talented managers soon found themselves making ineffective decisions, and would continue to take on more control in an effort to fix things. It has been said that as things got out of control, the best fix (and cover up for poor decisions) was the corporate reorganization. Reorganization would temporarily fix major problems by focusing everyone on other problems created by the reorganization. A common management philosophy is that the manager must make all decisions since they are in the best position to see the overall situation of the company.

Communication

The position used for communication in the traditional model is the "need to know only" basis for all levels. Managers would limit information to employees believing that they did not need to know more than the requirements of their specific job. This permeated throughout the organization so information flow was restricted in the downward direction. An interesting side note to communication is the management style coupled with the command and control mentality had a "shoot the messenger attitude" regarding any negative sounding information. So upward information was restricted by the lower levels that modified the "need to know only" philosophy to an "only give you what you want to hear" approach. Later in the cycle, these actions lead to silo effects and the development of a highly efficient bureaucracy movement in organizations.

Selling

Since the major theme is to persuade, the sales organizations were designed to "push" products or services down the channels. This practice was very effective during the economic growth times when demand outpaced supply.

So the companies developed a "build it and they will come" attitude and would aim to maximize their production. When the economic growth cycles would cool, then the management would tell the sales staff to go out and push sales to get rid of the inventory problem. It did not matter that their customers would have the inventory problem if the customer purchased more than they needed. The traditional model of selling was created to maximize product velocity. It assumed that anything could be sold at any time under any circumstances – just push it out the door. Using price as a means to move volume is a key element for the traditional sales organization. One additional point is the number of "lone wolf" type of sales people in this category. They prefer to work on their accounts and keep any information gained to themselves, resisting call reports and data input in customer databases. They will insist on being present whenever someone from their company visits one of their customers.

Key Selling Skills

The presentation model was the selling style of choice for the traditional model of selling. It was easier and more efficient to just tell the customer what is available than to find out if they preferred something else. Persuasion skills are important to the traditional sales person. They use these skills to handle objections and overcome barriers to buying. Product knowledge is considered a skill and is utilized as the weapon of choice by many traditional sellers. The most important skill for the traditional sales person is closing skill. How many closing techniques a salesperson could use in a typical sales presentation could be compared to the number of merit badges a Boy Scout could earn.

Structure

The structure of the organization would typically be centralized. This allowed for control of all elements of decision-making and gave more power to the managers. This structure has its origins in the military and was transferred to the corporate world. It worked quite well in the early and mid stages of the Industrial Revolution when employees were less educated and processes of operation were still being refined and organized. However, as the Industrial Age began to mature and employees were looking for new challenges in their job – tensions were created between staff and management. Some organizations claimed to decentralize, yet, they continued to control using new techniques of policies and procedures, work rules and standards, and even today's ISO series of written process rules.

Training & Development

The dollars spent for training and development in the traditional model company were focused on management and leadership training, product knowledge for sales people, and basic technical skills for new hires. Team building and communication skills development were limited to the top groups and were treated as too expensive or wasteful for the rank and file. In some cases, another situation exists whereby a training department has been formed to handle training in the organization. When this happens, a couple of factors become evident. The training budget is the first thing cut when economic conditions show signs of weakness. Another negative factor that shows up in training departments is the level of talent. Since traditional model managers assign a lower value to training, they tend to staff the training departments with people that have not been effective in other functional areas. This logic implies that anyone can train, just as anyone can sell, anyone can be a bank teller, and anyone can be a customer service person.

Performance

The traditional model companies are heavily influenced by the "get the numbers at all costs" business mentality. There is a tendency to heavily use promotions and price-cuts to move inventory (push) down the channels. People are treated like machine parts – if they wear out or miss standards, they can be replaced. Knowledge and information are not considered as important as immediate results. Matrices are implemented and refined to even tighter standards of performance as a means of controlling the personnel. In the end, it's all about pushing the product or service on the customer.

TRADITIONAL MODEL / PHILOSOPHY OF BUSINESS

Major Theme: *to Persuade*
Focused on: *Product / Service - Internal*
Management Style: *Command & Control*
Communication: *Limited, Need to Know Only*
Selling Strategy: *Push - use lone wolf sales people*
Key Selling Tactic: *Presentation Model - "Telling"*
Structure: *Centralized*
Training: *Limited / Low Priority*
Performance: *Numbers Driven*

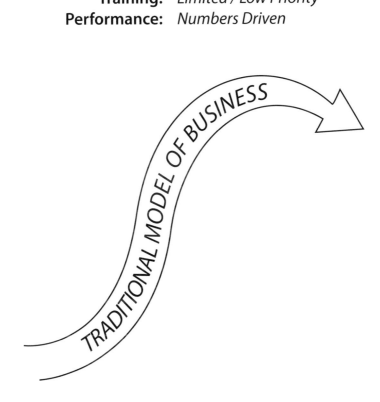

Graph One

New School

The Inneractive Model of Business

The *New School of Business*, which we now call the Inner*active* Model is the backbone of the Informational Age of Business. In order for the interactive model to operate at peak levels of effectiveness, certain "laws" of business or characteristics were developed for this model to survive or thrive in its world. Let's take a look at each factor within this model. *See Graph Two.*

Major Theme

The major theme within the Inneractive Model of Business is "to understand." From the top position on down, the people of the inneractive organization are using knowledge to get things done. Everyone in the organization is asking questions regarding customers, customer needs, what internal customers want and need, the processes used by the company, and the company's strategy. Effectiveness is the name of the game since the manager and employees know that no one person or group possesses all the answers, and time is the most important asset that few people have enough of these days. Questioning is the tactic of choice and is used by management to understand what is happening in their organizations, and sales people are using questions to understand and know their customers needs.

Focus

The major focus is on the company's customer. Using this strategy or tactic insures that everything revolves around the customer and the product or service needed by the customer. The combination of the "to understand" theme coupled with the focus being placed upon the company's customers, leads to an attitude of "We want to partner with you and develop win-win environments." This combination serves organizations well during all economic times, due to the fact that the closeness to the customer creates more accurate forecasts of projected demand and needed supply levels. Companies adopt "just-in-time" processes to minimize inventory, increase financial results using velocity of inventory turns, and only produce enough to satisfy their customer demands. Customer centric attitudes influence priorities on both managers and staff. Effectiveness becomes more important in the decision making process and information is shared with more people.

Management Style

Participatory Leadership is the most popular management method of the inneractive company. Since the economic environment is more complex and more choices are available today, a participatory style is necessary for the best managers. Managers are finding that the speed of change and the rapid increase in information have forced them to seek improved methods of staying current on the important information and delegating decision points to lower levels within the organization for timely decisions that impact customers. Committees and teams have taken on new roles and responsibilities in this new economic environment. Slow moving decision processes have eliminated certain competitors in today's markets. Managers are expected to mentor and coach their direct reports to accelerate the learning curve within organizations. While consensus decisions have proven to create some inefficiencies, multiple source input into the decision making process have improved the effectiveness of manager's decisions and actions.

Communication

The position used for communication in the inneractive model is held by the need for open and honest communication at all levels. Issues are discussed, dialogued, debated, and diagrammed by the people that the issue will impact. Changes are created by the people that they will impact; this creates a sense of involvement and commitment to the solution. Opinions are openly sought out for honest dialogue looking for synergies for alternative solutions to problems and challenges. Information flows in all directions and is not limited by any level of management. Bureaucracy has a short life span in the inneractive company.

Selling

Since the major theme is to understand, the sales organizations are designed to "pull" products or services through the channels. This practice is very effective during all economic cycles where demand is matched to supply. This method of selling demands the coordination and alignment of the sales and marketing functions to enhance brand and positioning strategies. The inneractive selling model was created to optimize product and service for numerous customer niches. It assumes that the best method of selling is to have the customer pulling products and services through the various channels identified. Another element of the inneractive selling model is the use of team selling, whereby the sales person actually becomes an account coordinator for multi-tasking of personnel in the selling process.

Key Selling Skills

The learning model is the selling style of choice for the inneractive model of selling. It requires more in-advance planning than the traditional model, since the sales person needs to identify what information is required for qualifying the customers' needs. Questioning skills are very important to the inneractive sales person. They use this skill to gain rapport with the customer, build trust in the offering, and discover problems and the consequences of these problems for the customer. Closing skills are less important due to the level of honest communication in the sales process that is designed to eliminate or minimize objections by discussing them up front. A key factor for sales success is the total involvement of the customer in the process, which increases their level of commitment to the salesperson's offering. The mark of an excellent sales person is the amount of detailed information he or she possesses about his or her customers.

Structure

The structure of the organization is typically de-centralized. This demands the use of empowered and responsible employees who are capable of performing at high levels. In some companies this de-centralized structure takes teamwork to new levels of effectiveness. Self-managing teams are the ultimate goal of some of these organizations because management knows that the team members are in a better position to serve their customers – both internally and externally. Trust based organizations are easily recognized by the lack of slogans, rules protecting the company, and procedures that limit the flexibility of employees making decisions that involve the customer.

Training & Development

The dollars spent for training and development in the inneractive model company are focused on improving performance at all levels of the organization. The types of training and development topics are expansive and provide specific improvement in the people skills of employees. The performance research has shown that emotional intelligence in the work place is critical to consistent high performance. Therefore, learning takes a higher priority in the corporation. This learning covers topics from person-al development, effective communication, team building, conflict resolution, leadership including personal leadership, and life-work balance. Since the inneractive model places a high value on people for their knowledge, experiences, and growth possibilities, development processes are more mainstream and are harder to eliminate during economic downturns. In fact, these organizations realize that the best times for training and developing their people are during these economic downturns. As the economy improves, their people are better prepared to handle the faster pace of business and usually are more skilled than their competitors. This focus on people actually creates a competitive advantage in the marketplace for these companies.

Performance

The leadership influences the inneractive model by driving the concept of "Hard on performance and soft on people." This concept ensures that people are accountable for their productivity and results, all while being dealt with in fair and humane ways. Performance goals are established for each person and team within the organization, as well as action plans for achieving those goals. Accountability sessions are held on a predetermined schedule. These companies also use Performance or Productivity Improvement Processes to insure the proper development of the talents necessary for high performance. These sessions are generally separate from salary or pay level discussions.

The key is to generate high performance from highly self-motivated individuals who choose to become part of a team effort. The teamwork increases both productivity and leverage within the organization and carries the organization to the next level.

INNERACTIVE MODEL / PHILOSOPHY OF BUSINESS

Graph Two

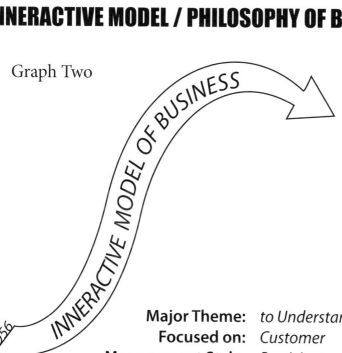

Major Theme:	*to Understand*
Focused on:	*Customer*
Management Style:	*Participatory*
Communication:	*Open & Honest*
Selling Strategy:	*Pull - Team Based*
Key Selling Tactic:	*Questioning - Learning*
Structure:	*Decentralized*
Training:	*Extensive / High Priority*
Performance:	*People / Talent Driven*

	TRADITIONAL	INNERACTIVE
Major Theme	*To Persuade*	*To Understand*
Focus	*Product / Service - Internal*	*Customer*
Management Style	*Command & Control*	*Participatory*
Communication	*Limited, Need to Know Only Basis*	*Open & Honest*
Selling Strategy	*Push - Use Lone Wolf Sales Person*	*Pull - Team Based*
Key Selling Tactics	*Presentation Model - "Telling"*	*Questioning - Learning*
Structure	*Centralized*	*Decentralized*
Training	*Limited / Low Priority*	*Extensive / High Priority*
Performance	*Numbers Driven*	*People / Talent Driven*

Conclusion

Experience Tells Us

Our experience working with sales teams from several industries has shown that the Traditional Model and the Inneractive Model are very much alive today. In fact, since they are running parallel to each other with their "S Curve" or wave theory (as shown on Graph 3) they are co-creating confusion and opportunity. The confusion is coming in the form of identifying who is on which curve. When sales people are presented with this information, they immediately recognize that some customers are Traditional model customers and some are Inneractive model customers. In fact, they then begin to describe how they have different managers, at different levels, within their own companies on different curves.

The Traditional and Inneractive Models describe what is driving different industries, companies, managers, and sales team individuals. These two models are the causality for the different actions taken by individuals within the same company; that, when examined shows direct contradiction of strategies, tactics, directives, or methods of execution. This becomes evident when formal discussions are raised to identify which model the company needs to embrace for its future success. However, these discussions are usually highly emotional due to the strong belief factors that are embraced by the individuals involved. It takes time for the total conversation to move to a specific model due to the emotions and beliefs that people possess. Just like coaching philosophies, old habits are hard to abandon and the new habits hard to begin. The most difficult thing for people to do in any organization is to unlearn old habits.

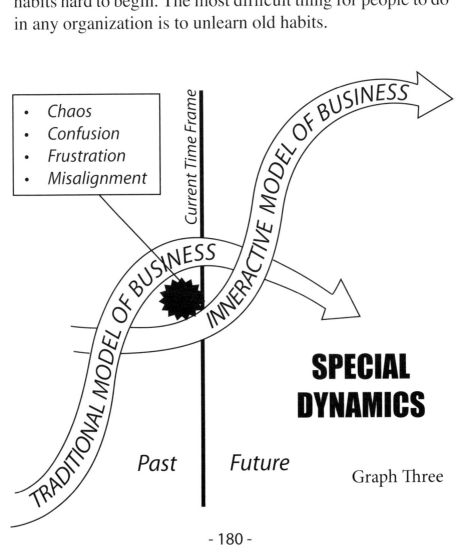

SPECIAL DYNAMICS

Graph Three

Special Situation for Sales Team Success

One thing that we have as a constant when using the two models, is the relationships of the sales person's model of selling, selling success, and the types of customers that they successfully sell. As we scouted out this knowledge with sales managers from several different industries, the information was the same. The model of selling that the sales person uses impacts their success levels and is a good indicator of whom will have the largest number of customers. The results of this knowledge clearly indicate the importance of getting the sales person on the inneractive curve.

First, in reviewing the levels of success within sales teams, the sales managers found that if a sales person used the traditional model of selling that 80-90% of their customers were also using the traditional model. An additional factor for sales managers: these sales people were the most active in asking for price concessions or discounts and as a group had lower gross margins on their sales volume. Also, the sales managers found little evidence of these sales people having customers who were considered to be on the inneractive model curve.

When the sales managers reviewed the sales levels of people who were positioned on the inneractive model of selling curve, they found most of their high performers. The sales managers found that the high performers had both customer models on their customer list, and had good volume from both groups while driving a higher margin on their sales volume. While they had traditional customers, they preferred to deal with their inneractive customer base and actively seek out inneractive customers in the marketplace using ideal customer profiles.

What caused this difference in customer base for these sales people and why did the interactive sales person have near equal weight distribution of traditional and inneractive customers? Actually, it was easy to discover the differentiator using questions and reviewing all the data available.

The inneractive sales people, using the learning model of selling, uncovered which position the customer modeled using questions and observation. Thus, the sales person using the inneractive model would change their offering to match the customer's needs. On the other hand, the traditional sales person would not learn very much using the presentation model. The inneractive model customer would reject the traditional sales person by using the "your price is too high" response to end the sales process. The inneractive model customer wants a sales person who is truly interested in helping or assisting the customer – not someone that only wants to push a sale.

The sales managers reported that their best sales people used the inneractive model of selling. An interesting note from the sales managers regarding the traditional sales people on their teams indicated three critical issues. First, some of the successful traditional sales people had not added any new business in several years and the sales managers indicated that while successful today, if anything happened to a couple of their key accounts that the sales person would be in serious trouble. Second, several of the traditional sales people were problematic, in that they appeared to have lost their motivation and were considered "prima donnas" or just plain old problem children in the eyes of their manager. The third element the sales managers raised was that the traditional sales people were vocal about pricing – in a downward direction. Thus, the sales managers were not looking at this group of sales people to lead their company into the future. The sales managers began to think about how they could find more inneractive sales people for their teams!

In summary, there are two economic philosophies running in tandem. Each has its own emphasis and priorities that are 180° in basic fundamentals. What is of concern is the vast majority of sales development is focused on the Traditional Model. This is a problem today for sales professionals and will continue to be a problem until sales executives and managers, who learned to sell under the old Traditional Model, understand the new model of selling. Until then, there will be added stress and lost opportunities. While it is true that Traditional customers expect to be sold in a traditional manner, sales individuals and teams have successfully differentiated themselves in the market place. In doing so, they have created a competitive advantage. They also understand that the structures of their offers change as they recognize which model the customer is operating within. This goes against the "one size fits all" sales strategies and sales team development practices.

So, how do you deal with this complexity? Simplify your processes by understanding how the "Three Games of Selling" open the future for dynamic gains in sales success. Give your sales team the ability to score from anywhere on the field – just like the best college football teams. Enable your teammates and playmakers to Make It Happen!

Appendix

Worksheets

Ideal Customer Worksheet

1.   List your best customers.

   _____

   _____

   _____

2.   Describe the traits and characteristics of your best customers.

   _____

   _____

   _____

3.   List your worst customers (problems, lack of respect, way they treat you and your company, etc)

   _____

   _____

   _____

4.   Describe the traits and characteristcs of your "worst customers" list.

   _____

   _____

   _____

5.   Describe an ideal customer - using the information gathered from your best and worst traits. *Reverse the content for your worst customers list into positives.*

   _____

   _____

   _____

   _____

   _____

Competitor Matrix Worksheet

	Your Company	Competitor A	Competitor B	...
Strengths ↑ / ↓ Weaknesses				

* Use as general competitor analysis on Product or Service comparisons.

** Compare customers to find target market

ABOUT THE AUTHOR

Voss W. Graham

Voss W. Graham is the CEO and Senior Business Advisor for InnerActive Consulting Group, Inc located in Cordova, TN. He has been an entreprenuer since 1983. He started his consulting career as a turnaround expert - helping organizations to transistion from near bankruptcy back to success. It was during this period of time, that he learned about the power of effective leadership. In the late eighties, he added training and development to his company. His company was a leading distribuor for Brian Tracy Learning Systems for over six years - focusing on sales team development and personal leadership growth.

Additional services offered by InnerActive Consulting Group, Inc. include assessments and selection processes, national account sales team development, strategic focus for executives and sales teams, effective communication for results, and "get you promoted" coaching.

He is available for consulting, executive coaching, sales team development, and assessing the quality of sales teams. Visit the consulting websites.
www.inneractiveconsulting.com
www.hiringsaleswinners.com

For online training and development, visit these websites:
www.theleadershipbuilder.com
www.masteryofsales.com

For Keynote or content presentations. A content expert without the ego! Visit this website:
www.vossgraham.com